MORE THAN YOU IMAGINE

Dear Mary,

May you accept your giftedness joyfully
as you pray these exercises.

Sabino S.J

A Journey with People of Faith

MORE THAN
YOU IMAGINE

Salvino Briffa, SJ

ALBA·HOUSE   NEW·YORK

SOCIETY OF ST. PAUL, 2187 VICTORY BLVD., STATEN ISLAND, NEW YORK 10314

Dedicated to

the Church, the Society of Jesus

and

my parents who parented me

into

the person I am

today.

Library of Congress Cataloging-in-Publication Data

Briffa, Salvino.
    More than you imagine : a journey with people of faith / by
    Salvino Briffa.
         p.   cm.
    1. Bible — Biography — Meditations.   I. Title.
    ISBN 0-8189-0553-0
    BS571.B68   1989   89-196
    220'.9'2 — dc19   CIP

Designed, printed and bound in the United States of
America by the Fathers and Brothers of the
Society of St. Paul, 2187 Victory Boulevard,
Staten Island, New York 10314, as part of their
communications apostolate.

© *Copyright 1989 by the Society of St. Paul*

Printing Information:

Current Printing - first digit 1 2 3 4 5 6 7 8 9 10 11 12

Year of Current Printing - first year shown
  1989   1990   1991   1992   1993   1994   1995   1996

ACKNOWLEDGMENTS

I would like to thank:

The many retreatants and directees who inspired me by sharing their spiritual journeys and who encouraged me to write this book.

The Detroit Jesuit Provincial Assistants who reviewed the manuscript and offered me valuable suggestions.

Sr. Patricia Hergenroether, S.S.J. for her patient reading, correction and evaluation of the manuscript.

Mrs. Terri LaRoque and Mrs. Ruth Wall for their gracious and excellent typing skills.

All scriptural references are taken from:
The New American Bible, St. Joseph Edition, 1970.

ABBREVIATIONS

OLD TESTAMENT

Genesis	Gn	Proverbs	Pr
Exodus	Ex	Ecclesiastes	Ec
Leviticus	Lv	Song of Songs	Sg
Numbers	Nb	Wisdom	Ws
Deuteronomy	Dt	Sirach	Si
Joshua	Jos	Isaiah	Is
Judges	Jg	Jeremiah	Jr
Ruth	Rt	Lamentations	Lm
1 Samuel	1 S	Baruch	Ba
2 Samuel	2 S	Ezekiel	Ezk
1 Kings	1 K	Daniel	Dn
2 Kings	2 K	Hosea	Ho
1 Chronicles	1 Ch	Joel	Jl
2 Chronicles	2 Ch	Amos	Am
Ezra	Ezr	Obadiah	Ob
Nehemiah	Ne	Jonah	Jon
Tobit	Tb	Micah	Mi
Judith	Jdt	Nahum	Na
Esther	Est	Habakkuk	Hab
1 Maccabees	1 M	Zephaniah	Zp
2 Maccabees	2 M	Haggai	Hg
Job	Jb	Malachi	Ml
Psalms	Ps	Zechariah	Zc

NEW TESTAMENT

Matthew	Mt	1 Timothy	1 Tm
Mark	Mk	2 Timothy	2 Tm
Luke	Lk	Titus	Tt
John	Jn	Philemon	Phm
Acts	Ac	Hebrews	Heb
Romans	Rm	James	Jm
1 Corinthians	1 Cor	1 Peter	1 P
2 Corinthians	2 Cor	2 Peter	2 P
Galatians	Gal	1 John	1 Jn
Ephesians	Ep	2 John	2 Jn
Philippians	Ph	3 John	3 Jn
Colossians	Col	Jude	Jude
1 Thessalonians	1 Th	Revelation	Rv
2 Thessalonians	2 Th		

FOREWORD

THIS BOOK is meant to be prayed and not read. In order to have a fruitful prayer, you may want to tape the exercise to be prayed beforehand so as to avoid the distraction of reading. Another suggested method is to read one or two paragraphs at a time and then let your imagination activate your heart and mind, allowing the prayer to flow naturally. Some people like to read verse by verse slowly and, as they read, come in touch with the truthfulness that the reality within unfolds.

The following are some practical suggestions for a fruitful prayer experience. I suggest that:

- You choose the place you like most for your prayer.
- If you are sitting, keep your head straight with the trunk of your body.
- Quieten yourself through a breathing or relaxing exercise. For five minutes:

    - Breathe in and out and become aware of the rhythm of your breathing.
    - Feel the breath cool as you inhale, warm as you exhale.
    - Experience the body relaxing and your heart and mind emptying themselves from thoughts and feelings.
    - Start the prayer by letting what you heard or read activate your imagination as it touches the reality stored in the silent depth of your being.

- Accept and take mental note of whatever unfolds itself to you and refrain from judging or censoring what is unfolded.
- Relish fully what the imagination presents to you and move on without any anxiety to further prayer.
- As you pray, become aware of whatever is happening within you by taking note of feelings, thoughts, memories, etc.
- End the prayer exercise gently.
- When the prayer is over, take a few moments to check what the imagination has unfolded to you. Become aware of the experiences you have had and check what they tell you about your daily behavior and attitudes.
- As you accept all this, see what the prayer is inviting you to do, and respond as naturally and generously as you can.
- End the prayer with a loving dialogue with any Person of the Triune God.

TABLE OF CONTENTS

INTRODUCTION xiii

OLD TESTAMENT EXEMPLARS

  1. Abraham   3
  2. Moses   6
  3. Judith 10
  4. Ruth 13
  5. Esther 17
  6. Isaac 20
  7. King David 23
  8. Jonathan 27
  9. Isaiah 29
10. Jeremiah 33
11. Hannah 36
12. Job 39
13. Jonah 42
14. Eleazar 45
15. Ezekiel 48
16. The Ideal Wife 51
17. The Maccabean Mother 54

NEW TESTAMENT PATTERNS

18. John the Baptist 59
19. Mary, Our Lady 62
20. Joseph 65

21. Peter 69
22. The Beloved Disciple 72
23. Matthew 76
24. Thomas 79
25. Paul 82
26. Martha 84
27. Mary (Martha's Sister) 88
28. Nicodemus 91
29. The Would-Be Disciples 94
30. The Seventy-Two Disciples 97
31. The Farsighted Steward 100
32. Zechariah 103
33. Pilate 106
34. The Bent-Over Woman 109
35. The Grateful Leper 113
36. The Repentant Criminal 116
37. The Penitent Woman 118
38. Simon, The Pharisee 121
39. The Widow of Naim 124
40. The Pharisee and The Tax Collector 128
41. Zacchaeus 131
42. The Rich Man 134
43. The Rich Fool 137
44. Mary Magdalene 140

GUARDIANS

45. Raphael 147
46. Gabriel 149
47. Michael 152
48. Guardian Angel 155
49. Crowned With Glory and Honor 158
50. Be On Your Guard 161

INTRODUCTION

WHEN *That I May See* was published, I was frequently asked: "When is the second book coming?" My first reaction was that one book is enough. Yet as I kept hearing the same question, I felt invited and challenged to write again.

My first book was so well received and the remarks about its method of prayer so positive, I decided to have the second book be a continuation of it. In fact, I can call it Volume Two. Imagination helps the praying person discover the full truthfulness about oneself. I turned my imagination toward Scripture because retreatants and directees so often find God and their True Self in the Scriptures.

This book is the fruit of my reflection on people with whom I come in contact. As I continue to offer spiritual companionship and direct retreats, I am always fascinated with the richness of each person. In our faith journey, we experience strengths and weaknesses, being in progress and being at a standstill, generosity and selfishness. Such characteristics are present in each unique, human person. Because of this richness, we are often confused and question our spiritual growth. As I bring these feelings, reflections and imagination to my prayer, I cannot help comparing people with some personages in the Scriptures. The figures we pray with in the Bible are people like us, blessed and broken, human and spiritual. It is these reflective comparisons that gave birth to this book.

I chose to write about people in the Scriptures because by praying with them, one experiences consolation and encouragement as one realizes that these saints passed through the same journey of doubts, failures and hope that we are experiencing today.

This book deals with fifty personages in the Scriptures. Through active imagination, you are helped to discover similarities with the persons with whom you have prayed. This unfolds to you the richness of God's love. Each prayer exercise is the fruit of my prayerful reflection helped by a practical application to life situations.

The book is divided into three sections. The first two sections present personages who can be models and patterns for a peaceful journey of spiritual growth. The Bible offers us people who, like us, experienced similar situations that can be daring or frightening. My desire is that as you pray with each Scriptural personage, you will discover the wonderful masterpiece God intends for you to become as you accept the many gifts with which you are blessed.

The third section presents the archangels and angels as guides in the process of fulfilling our Christian journey in search for Truth. I am sure the Psalmist admired these angels and reflected on them since he could sing: "You made him little less than an angel and crowned him with glory and honor." (Psalm 8:6)   May you have a similar experience as you pray this section of the book.

This book would be too monotonous if you just read it. It is meant to be prayed and reflected upon, one exercise after another. You may use it during a retreat or on days of prayer. If helpful, you may want to use it once or twice a week during your daily formal prayer time.

My desire is, that as you pray this book, you will discover and accept the many qualities of each Scriptural personage. At the end of the book you will be able to experience God's unconditional love and this will be enough reason for you to live a life of praise and gratitude to God who "has made you little less than an angel and crowned you with glory and honor." (cf. Psalm 8:6)   It is this discovery or experience that I had in mind when I titled the book: *More Than You Imagine*, taken from Ephesians 3:20.

OLD TESTAMENT EXEMPLARS

1.
ABRAHAM

(Genesis 12, 13, 15, 17, 21)

I INVITE YOU to prayerfully journey with Abraham, our Father in Faith and let this journey draw you close to God and deepen your faith.

The call from God that made Abram into Abraham is a call in faith, a series of leaps in the dark that were always abundantly blessed.

"The Lord said to Abram: 'Go forth from the land of your kinsfolk and from your father's house to a land that I will show you.' Abram went as the Lord directed him . . . [he] was seventy-five years old . . ." (Gn 12:1, 4)

Like Abram, you, too, have been called to put your trust in God:

- How old were you when God called you to follow Him?
- Was your age then a hindrance in following the Lord?
- Where and for what did the Lord call you?
- Did God's call imply leaving the safety of your home, the familiarity of your state or the pride of your country?
- What obstacles and hindrances, fears and anxieties had you to work with to do what the Lord asked of you?
- Get in touch with your faith-journey as the Lord has directed you.

When Abram settled in Canaan, the Lord said to him: "All the land that you see I will give to you and your descendants

forever. I will make your descendants like the dust of the earth."
(Gn 13:15-16)   Recall your call and response to God:

- What promises did God make to you when He called you?
- What do the vast land and the numerous descendants represent in your call?
- Do you see in your inspirations and feelings, then, any of God's promises?
- Was it hard for you to believe that God would be true to His promises?
- How great was your trust in God then?

Abram puts his trust in God and God made a Covenant with him. "Fear not, Abram! I am your shield; I will make your reward very great." (Gn 15:1)   "No, that one shall not be your heir, your own issue shall be your heir." (15:4)   "My covenant with you is this: You are to become the father of a host of nations. No longer shall you be called Abram; your name shall be Abraham, for I am making you the father of a host of nations. I will render you exceedingly fertile . . . I will maintain my covenant with you and your descendants . . . as an everlasting pact, to be your God." (17:4-7)

It was hard for Abraham to believe that God's promise would come true:

- How could a man, a hundred years old and a woman ninety years old bear a son?
- How could Abraham and Sarah believe they would be "exceedingly fertile"?
- Even though they laughed at themselves, they trusted in the Lord.

"Abraham put his faith in the Lord who credited it to him as an act of righteousness." (Gn 15:6)

Become aware of some difficult calls in your life. Calls that shook your faith, questioned your common sense or even challenged the natural flow of nature:

- What were these calls by God?
- What covenant did God make with you then?
- What reasons and objections made you question, doubt and challenge God?
- How did your trust in God come about?
- Who and what helped you to put aside all natural thinking, reasoning and feeling and accept that inner movement that made you "put your faith in the Lord"?
- Take a few moments of prayer and relive this sacred moment of faith in the Lord, your God.

God always outdoes us in generosity. Abraham trusted in God and was greatly blessed as God fulfilled His covenant. What seemed impossible happened.

"I am making you the father of a host of nations." (Gn 17:5) "Your wife Sarah is to bear you a son, and you shall call him Isaac." (17:19) "Sarah became pregnant and bore Abraham a son in his old age . . . Abraham gave the name Isaac to this son of his whom Sarah bore him." (21:2-3)

As you come in touch with your faith-filled responses to God, look at your past:

- How has God rewarded your trust and faith in Him?
- What kind of reward are you now enjoying?
- Is this reward spiritual, physical, emotional, psychological?
- As you count your blessings and feel the wonder of God's love for you, spend a moment of praise and glory to God for making His promises come true in you.

Abraham's faith was critically tested when God asked him to sacrifice his son, Isaac. Abraham loved God so much that he obeyed promptly.

"Do not do the least thing to him. I know now how devoted you are to God, since you did not withhold from me your own beloved son." (Gn 22:12)

Before you end this exercise, look back at your life and remember the times when your love and faith in God were truly tested:

- What was the test of your fidelity to God's love?
- What were you asked to sacrifice to prove your love for God?
- What struggles did you encounter in proving your love for and faith in God?
- How was the Lord present during all this?
- What helped you to say a full yes to God even though it hurt?
- Take a few moments and:

  - Thank God for the gifts of faith and trust you have.
  - Thank Him for the many generous responses you gave to His calls.
  - Ask Him to strengthen your faith so as to continue seeing in your loving responses "an act of righteousness and salvation."

- When you are ready, gently end the exercise.

2.
MOSES

(Exodus 3-34)

As you journey with Moses in this prayer, I invite you to draw parallels between him and you, his mission and your mission.

Moses experienced his call as he watched the burning bush. "I must go over to look at this remarkable sight and see why the bush is not burned." (Ex 3:3)

Become aware of your mission in life and go back to the time and place when you first heard the call:

- Where were you when you first experienced the Lord calling you?
- What were you doing then? Praying? Celebrating life? Grieving? Searching?
- Were you alone or with others?
- Was the call gentle and subtle or direct and clear?
- What was your immediate response?

As Moses responded to the call, God gave him a tough mission to fulfill. ". . . the cry of the Israelites has reached me, and I have truly noted that the Egyptians are oppressing them. Come, now! I will send you to Pharaoh to lead my people, the Israelites, out of Egypt." (Ex 3:9-10)

Because of your openness to the Lord's call, Jesus offered you your mission. Prayerfully, go back to the early stages of your mission and become aware of strengths and weaknesses at work in your response:

- Were you clear from the start what your mission was and what it implied?
- Did you accept your mission quickly and generously or did you have to pray, discern and struggle to experience clarity and certainty?
- Did you experience your mission as a challenge or threat, something to look forward to or something you dreaded thinking about?
- As you realized this was God's will for you, did you, like Moses, doubt and fear your inadequacy? "If the Israelites would not listen to me, how can it be that Pharaoh will listen to me, poor speaker that I am!" (Ex 6:12)

- What fears and doubts did you then experience?
- How incompetent and inadequate did you feel?
- Was this inadequacy the result of mistrust in God or the result of a poor self-image you then had?
- What made you say a ''Full Yes'' to Jesus, even though you doubted and feared your faithfulness and generosity?
- Take some time and thank Jesus for the gifts you then used to accept your mission.

God chose Moses because He loved him dearly. Moses, in turn, was generous enough to pay the double price that was asked of him in fulfilling his mission.

Moses faced Pharaoh's hard-heartedness with wonderful patience and strong belief that God was his Rock of Safety.

We repeatedly read in Exodus that Pharaoh remained obstinate and would not listen to Moses.   (Ex 7:22; 8:11, 28; 9:7, 12, 34-35; 10:20, 27 . . .)

In dealing with Pharaoh's arrogance, Moses kept his cool, acted humbly and patiently and persevered till the end because he trusted that God would help him complete his mission.

The faithful fulfillment of your mission implies moments of struggle and anxious decisions. As you look at your experiences:

- Who and what are the Pharaohs in your life? Name them.
- Where and how do these Pharaohs attack and challenge you?
- How do you react to these challenges of the Pharaohs within and outside you?
- Are you strong in facing opposition and threats or do you falter in trust, courage and self-esteem?
- What role does Jesus play in you and in the Pharaohs that attack you?

Dealing with the criticism and instability of the Israelites was another price Moses paid for his faithfulness to his mission.

The Israelites repeatedly grumbled against God, criticized Him, disobeyed Him and lost faith in His guidance. "Would that we had died at the Lord's hand in the land of Egypt . . . but you had to lead us into the desert to make the whole community die of famine!" (Ex 16:3, cf. 17:3)

Moses responded to this criticism with love and compassion to the extent that he interceded for the people with God: "Let your blazing wrath die down; relent in punishing your people." (Ex 32:12)

As you look at the people with whom you share your ministry and at those whom you serve:

- What difficulties do you face from family and staff members?
- With what obstacles and hindrances do the people you serve burden you?
- Is your response to these obstacles a feeling of anger and a sense of giving up or is it a deepening of compassion and forgiveness?
- Moses prayed, "Pardon, then, the iniquity of this people in keeping with your great kindness, even as you have forgiven them from Egypt until now." (Nb 14:19)
- What is YOUR prayer in the midst of adversity, obstacles and criticism as you continue to be faithful to your mission?

In carrying his cross Moses often felt anxious, angry and discouraged. Yet in his intimacy with God, he always unburdened his heart sincerely as a friend. "I am not able to carry all these people alone, the burden is too heavy for me. If you will deal thus with me, kill me at once, if I find favor in your sight that I may not see my wretchedness." (Nb 11:14-15)

- As you experience similar anxieties, anger, obstacles and discouragement in your mission, what is your approach to Jesus?
- Is Jesus a real friend whom you trust and with whom you can share whatever feelings you experienced?
- Or is your relationship with Jesus still legalistic, frail and formal?

Trials and criticism from the Israelites helped Moses to become an intimate friend of God, and "God made Moses hear His voice and led him into the dark cloud; face to face He gave him the commandments, a law that brings life and knowledge. . . ." (Si 45:5)

"The Lord used to speak to Moses face to face, as a man speaks to a friend . . . and behold the skin of his face shone. . . ." (Ex 33:11, 34:29)

Before you end this prayer, I invite you to become aware of your growth as you accept the many experiences that your mission and ministry in life offer you. As you accept the growth you experience in the different aspects of your life because of your faithfulness to your mission, spend a few moments in face to face dialogue with Jesus. Let Him inundate you with His life, love and joy so that, experiencing the radiance of these gifts in your being, you may be able to rest quietly and peacefully in the Lord. When you are ready, gently end the exercise.

3.
JUDITH

(Judith 8-16)

Note: It would be good to read Judith, chapters 8-16 before you pray the exercise.

JUDITH is an inspiration to all of us. She fought and overcame evil by using her giftedness in prayer and fasting. In this exercise, become aware of the evil in and around you. As you reflect on Judith's struggle with evil, get in touch with the ways the Lord calls you to struggle and overcome it.

Judith was an attractive woman, widowed when young, who possessed many riches. She "fasted all the days of her widowhood . . . and feared God with great devotion." (Jdt 8:6-8)   I invite you to reflect on your personality:

- What kind of person are you? Beautiful and attractive, handsome and rich or just an ordinary person enjoying the necessary comforts of life?
- How do you accept your riches and where do they lead you?
- Is God included among your personal riches?
- Is your relationship to God similar to Judith's (devotion-awe-prayer) or different?
- What place does God have in your life?

Being a God-fearing woman, Judith is saddened and angered that her people put God to the test. She exhorts them: ". . . we should be grateful to the Lord, our God who is putting us to the test . . . He has not tried us with fire . . . nor has He taken revenge upon us. It is by way of admonition that He chastises those who are close to Him." (Jdt 8:25-27)

In the quietness of your heart, look around you and become aware of the evil that surrounds you:

- Personally, how does the evil spirit tempt you?
- What are the evils to which you are attracted?
- What form does evil take in your family: financial, emotional, physical or moral?
- How does this evil affect your family members?
- Look beyond your family to your city or town. Where and how do you see the faces of evil?
- What do people tell you about their own evils?
- What do you see in addiction, violence, prostitution, murders?

As you experience this evil in and around you:

- Do you curse God for allowing this to happen?
- Do you accuse the people affected by evil and do you look down at them?
- Are you self-righteous? Do you ignore the situation? Have you given up hope?
- Or do you, like Judith, turn to God seeking forgiveness and healing?

Judith sought deliverance from the cruel Holofernes in prayer, fasting and penance. (Jdt 9) Her hope was in God who is the "helper of the oppressed, the supporter of the weak, the protector of the forsaken, the savior of those without hope." (9:11)

As you look at your struggle with evil, what do you see yourself doing to help yourself and others be delivered from it?

- Do you believe in prayer, penance and fasting as means of deliverance?
- Is your penance just an exterior show or does it affect your spirit?
- Are you satisfied with physical fasting or do you seek the fasting of the soul by tempering your anger, forgiving hurts and restraining your tongue?
- Is your prayer for deliverance from evil sincere, faith-filled and confident?
- As you come in touch with these spiritual disciplines, spend a few moments in loving dialogue with Jesus.

Persevering in prayer, penance and self-control, Judith used her beauty and wisdom to overcome Holofernes, the personification of evil. In her last struggle with evil she prayed: " 'Strengthen me this day, O God of Israel!' Then with all her might she struck him twice in the neck and cut off his head." (Jdt 13:7-8)

Judith's victory over and deliverance from evil are the result of persevering prayer and penance and the right use of her strengths. I invite you to look at the times when you experienced deliverance from evil, either in yourself or in others:

- Can you honestly say that deliverance came partly as a response to your prayer and penance?
- Have you ever helped others in evil situations to seek healing and purification by your example of a faith-filled and prayerful life?
- How strong is your belief in the efficacy of prayer?
- How do you use your natural qualities and acquired gifts to bring healing and peace in yourself and in others?

As Judith returned to her people carrying Holofernes' head, all the people worshipped God and blessed Judith for her upright life. (Jdt 13:17-20)

Before you end this exercise, take a few moments of loving dialogue with Jesus. Relive a touching moment in this very exercise and let Jesus tell you what you need to hear. Then, with Judith, offer Him your song of gratitude. (Jdt 16:1-17) When you are ready, gently end the exercise.

4.
RUTH

(Ruth 1-4)

IN THIS PRAYER, I invite you to get in touch with the first step of Ruth's call. Because of famine in Bethlehem, Naomi and her family traveled to Moab. There, Naomi's son, Chilion, married Ruth.

Take some time and reflect on your married life. As you go back to the stages of your marriage, consider:

- What were the first signs that God was calling you to the married life?
- What opinions, ideals, thoughts and feelings did you then have about marriage?
- What were the circumstances that led you to meet your spouse?

Now go back to the place and time when either of you proposed marriage:

- How was the proposal made and what feelings did you then experience?
- What reactions were you aware of then in you and in your partner?
- What certainty did you then have about a successful marriage?
- What strengths and weaknesses did you then see in yourself and in your partner?
- Were you aware of differences between you? How did you deal with them?
- What made you say YES to marriage?

After ten years, Ruth became a widow and she chose to remain with Naomi, her mother-in-law. As you experience the pain of separation in Ruth, look at your own marriage and become aware of:

- Pains and sufferings that you endured during your married life.
- Did these pains arise from natural causes, because of your spouse or because of your personality?
- What responses did you give to the different hurts and pains?
- Did these sufferings open negative wounds in you that led you to sharper sorrows?

- Or did you use them to redeem your marriage and to integrate your personality?
- As you look at the past, become aware of Jesus laboring in you and of your cooperation with Him. Spend a short time in loving dialogue with Him.

When Naomi was returning to Bethlehem and urged her daughters-in-law to return to their mother and seek remarriage, Ruth answered her, "Do not ask me to abandon or forsake you! For wherever you go I will go, wherever you lodge I will lodge; your people shall be my people, and your God my God." (Rt 1:16)

As you ponder on Ruth's faithfulness and respect for her mother-in-law, I invite you to relive difficult experiences in your married life:

- What is your relationship to your in-laws?
- How do you feel with differences in personalities, life-styles, family customs and social life?
- Do these differences enhance misunderstanding and create jealousies and divisions?
- Or do they purify your understanding and strengthen your loving union and respect for each other?
- Present these differences to Jesus and ask for healing, forgiveness and strength.

Living in Bethlehem with Naomi, Ruth worked hard to earn a living for herself and her mother-in-law. ". . . and ever since she came this morning she has remained here until now, with scarcely a moment's rest." (Rt 2:7) Ruth adapted herself to her new people and town by living in the present:

- How do you deal with weaknesses, changes and novelties in life?
- Do you live in the past, pitying yourself and wanting your children to be exactly like you in every way?

- Or are you open to changes, to new ideas and attitudes that make you and the whole family grow?
- Do you take changes and novelties as threats or as challenges to be faced with faith and trust?
- In the trivial family troubles and in your ordinary disagreements with your spouse, do you harbor anger, jealousy and hatred?
- Or do you honestly share your feelings, looking for solutions and peace of soul?

Ruth's efforts were highly rewarded. Boaz not only blessed Ruth saying, "May you receive a full reward from the Lord, the God of Israel," (Rt 2:12) but also agreed to marry her, "So be assured, daughter, I will do for you whatever you say; all my townspeople know you for a worthy woman." (3:11) By her marriage to Boaz, Ruth, a Moabite woman, entered into the ancestry of Jesus. Her son Obed was the father of Jesse, the father of David.

Take a few moments and, as you relive some of the meaningful mysteries of your life and the way that you grew because of the way you faced them:

- Thank Jesus for the gifts He shares with you in your personality.
- Relish the qualities you so often use to keep a healthy and joyful family spirit.
- Ask Jesus to strengthen you in moments of doubt, insecurity and struggle.
- Allow Him to bless you, encourage you and strengthen you as He tells you how pleased He is with you and with all you do to keep a peaceful and happy family. When you are ready, gently end the exercise.

5.
ESTHER

(Esther 2-10)

*Note: It would be good to read the book of Esther,
chapters 2-10 before you pray this exercise.*

The call of Esther to intercede for her people with King Ahasuerus is an example of a faith-filled and effective prayer. "Esther found favor in the eyes of all who saw her." (Est 2:15) "The king loved Esther more than all women, and she found grace and favor in his sight more than all virgins so that he set the royal crown on her head." (2:17)

I invite you to imagine Jesus in front of you and to get in touch with your relationship with Him. In the silence of your heart, become aware of:

- Your beauty, richness and strengths that make Jesus find favor and grace in you.
- Is the strength of your beauty physical, psychological or spiritual?
- What qualities within you cause Jesus to favor you more than others?
- How do you respond to Jesus finding such favor in you?
- Do you feel, like Esther, that Jesus is crowning you as queen or king in your own way?
- What does this crowning mean to your relationship with Jesus and with the people among whom you live?

Esther became queen at the right time and for the right purpose. When "Haman sought to destroy Mordecai and all the

Jews throughout the whole kingdom of Ahasuerus'' (Est 3:6),
''Mordecai asked Esther to go to the king to make supplication to
him and entreat him for her people'' (4:8): ''Who knows
whether you have come to the kingdom for such a time as
this?'' (4:14)

As you look at your personality, state in life, ministry and the
growth with which you have been blessed:

- What are the stages that led you to who and what you are today?
- What people, events and circumstances influenced you in this
  process of growth?
- Are you pleased with your responses and cooperation with Jesus'
  calls?
- How was Jesus present in each stage of growth as you heard His
  calls and responded to them?

As Esther listened to Mordecai's plea to entreat the king for
her people who were threatened by destruction, she experienced
the call to be the INTERCESSOR for her people. Accepting this
mission, she prepared by prayer and penance. ''. . . and Esther fled
to the Lord . . . covered her head with ashes and dirt . . . she utterly
humbled her body . . . and prayed to the Lord God of Israel.''
(Est C:12-14) She prayed, ''O God, whose might is over all,
hear the voice of the despairing and save us from the hands of
evildoers. And save me from my fear.'' (C:30)

Take a moment and become aware of your mission and
ministry:

- Where and to what ministry have your qualities and education
  brought you?
- To whom do you minister and what is your mission in life?
- How do the people to whom you minister call you to prayer for
  self, for them and for others?
- From your experiences, do you feel invited, obliged or pressured
  to intercede for people in need?

- How do the evils of war, terminal diseases, racism, greed, etc. affect your prayer?
- Is your prayer of supplication faith-filled?
- Is your prayer accompanied by some kind of penance?
- What strength do you gain from your prayer?

Because of her sincere love for her people and her deep faith in the compassionate God of Israel, Esther, spiritually strengthened, entered into the king's presence for her special request. "I ask that my life be given at my petition, and my people at my request. For we are sold, I and my people, to be destroyed, to be slain and to be annihilated." (Est 7:3-4)

As you look at your relationship with Jesus, consider:

- Is your prayer to Jesus faith-filled so that He will grant you your requests?
- Is your love for the people for whom you pray sincere, true and honest?
- Or are you indifferent to the needs of the people around you because you are rich enough and self-sufficient?
- What makes you courageous enough to enter God's presence and intercede for people in need?

Right now, become still and silent. Let people whom you really love and care for, and who are in need of help, show their faces to you. As different individuals and groups of people come to your heart and mind:

- Present them to Jesus the Comforter and Savior.
- Ask Him, entreat Him and plead with Him for their healing, safety and salvation.
- Offer them and their needs one by one, group by group to Jesus.

- Use your qualities that make you favored by Jesus in your prayer of petition and supplication.
- And experience Jesus bringing relief, healing, spiritual freedom and salvation to these people.

As you experience the power of your faith-filled and loving prayer to Jesus, end the exercise with a few moments of grateful celebration of the God who "has made this day to be a joy to His chosen people instead of a day of destruction for them." (Est E:21)

6.
ISAAC
(Genesis 17, 21-26)

ISAAC is a man born in fulfillment of God's promise when his parents were very old and his mother was considered infertile.

"Sarah bore Abraham a son . . . Abraham gave the name Isaac to this son of his whom Sarah bore him." (Gn 21:2-3)

In imagination, go back to your birth and what you know about it and become aware of:

- What were your parents like then: their ages, beliefs, convictions, jobs, etc.
- Was there anything special about your birth?
- What do you know about the circumstances of your conception and birth?
- Like Isaac, are you an only child, the eldest in the family, a fulfillment of some promise?
- What blessings do you see in your birth?
- How was God present in the circumstances of your birth?

Isaac's life was accompanied by a promise from God. "Him also will I bless; he shall give rise to nations, and rulers of peoples shall issue from him." (Gn 17:16)   In spite of this promise, God tested the faith of Abraham very seriously. "Then God said: 'Take your son Isaac, your only one, whom you love, and go to the land of Moriah. There you shall offer him up as a holocaust on a height that I will point out to you.' " (22:2)

Even though the testing was very hard and Abraham was confused — "Son, God himself will provide the sheep for the holocaust" (Gn 22:8) — yet he did what the Lord commanded him. (22:3-14)

Isaac, in turn, accepted to become the holocaust. He himself carried the wood and allowed his father to tie him up "and put him on top of the wood on the altar." (22:9)

As you become present to this awesome act of faith, get in touch:

- With Abraham's thoughts and feelings as he accepts God's command.
- With the confusion in Abraham's heart and mind as he realizes that:
  - Isaac is his only son, born when he was one hundred years old.
  - God promised him a great posterity and now is asking for the destruction of the source of all his hope.
  - Sarah became fertile precisely because God wanted her to give birth to Isaac.

Become Isaac, God's promised gift and requested holocaust. Listen to Abraham calling you to accompany him to offer the sacrifice to the Lord. As you walk toward the place of sacrifice, let your mind wonder at the mystery of the moment:

- What thoughts cross your mind as you walk to the place of sacrifice?

- What feelings arise within you as you do not have the sacrificial victim?
- What do you say and do to Abraham and to God?

Now become aware of YOUR journey in faith:

- Have you ever experienced a call to sacrifice any aspect of yourself?
- Was this sacrifice asked of you:

  - At home, at work, in the Church?
  - Spiritually, emotionally, intellectually?

- What exactly were you asked to sacrifice?
- Become aware of the struggle you went through to come to a decision.
- Can you honestly call this a "crisis in faith"?
- What was the price you had to pay to prove your love for the Lord?
- Who was the Abraham, the exemplar of fidelity and generosity for you?
- Who was the saving angel in your crisis of faith?
- Take a moment and, as you relive the times of crisis in faith, let your heart find rest in the heart of Jesus, the reward of your faith.

God's promise to Abraham was fulfilled in Isaac in two ways:

1. Isaac married Rebekah, the woman of God's choice. "Here is Rebekah, ready for you; take her with you, that she may become the wife of your master's son, as the Lord has said." (Gn 24:51)

   Rebekah gave birth to twins (Esau and Jacob) representing two nations. "Two nations are in your womb . . . but one shall surpass the other, and the older shall serve the younger." (Gn 25:23) "I will bless you and multiply your descendants for the sake of my servant Abraham." (26:24)

2. Isaac prospered in the hands of the Lord. "He became richer and richer all the time, until he was very wealthy indeed." (26:13)

Become aware of God's promises to you and of His fidelity to your response in faith. Look at the times when you responded generously to God's calls, times when your faith and love cost you pain and self-denial. As you look back:

- How has the Lord rewarded you for all that you have given to Him?
- Name the rewards of God for you, accept them once more and be grateful.
- What growth, development or maturity do you see in you as a result of your faith?
- What makes you certain that it is not you but the Lord's gifts and rewards that are present in you?
- Take a few moments and, as you become aware of how much the Lord has blessed you:

    - Thank Him for all His gifts, especially faith, hope and love.
    - Join Isaac in thanking the Lord for all that He is and has done for you, as you worship Him in the sanctuary of your heart.

- When you are ready, gently end the exercise.

7.
KING DAVID
(1 Samuel 16-17; 2 Samuel 5-7)

Already from childhood, little David was chosen by God and called from tending his father's flock to shepherd God's people.

God told Samuel: ''I am sending you to Jesse of Bethlehem, for I have chosen my king from among his sons.'' (1 S 16:1) ''Then Samuel . . . anointed him in the midst of his brothers, and from that day on, the spirit of the Lord rushed upon him.'' (16:13)

David was the youngest of Jesse's children. He was not a warrior but a shepherd boy looking after his father's flock.

Look at your present family and work position and go back to the first stages of your growth and development:

- Who was in your family when you were born?
- How many children were there and where did you stand among them?
- Was your family then ordinarily well-established and secure or did you have to struggle because of depression, war or poverty?
- What first signs did you have that God chose you and called you to be what you have become?
- David was anointed king among his brothers. Do you have any experience of God putting a seal on your heart and making you what He wanted you to be?

David accepted God's choice and anointing and he was abundantly blessed in return:

- He fought with and killed the Philistine, Goliath, because he fought in the name of the Lord of hosts. (1 S 17:41-54)
- He carried out successfully every mission of King Saul. (1 S 18:5, 30)
- He was anointed king of Judah (2 S 2:4) and of Israel (2 S 5:3).

Look back at your early responses to God's call for you and reflect:

- Have you always cooperated with God's call?
- Were your responses always positive and God-centered even though you are weak?
- How has God rewarded you as you kept answering His call?

David prospered in life both as a father and as king. He was blessed with many children and surrounded by love (2 S 3:2-3) and he was victorious in many wars. (2 S 3, 8)

As you look at yourself today:

- Do you feel that God has blessed you?
- What about the love of your spouse and children?
- If a community person, of how many members can you say: "They really love me"?
- What about true and enduring friendships?
- Do you see God's protective love in your profession or ministry and in the stability of your life in general?

With all these rich blessings, David was always aware of God's love. He knew he was "God's Chosen" and, in return, he was a God-fearing man. David proved this fear of God when:

- He spared Saul's life, even though he could have killed him. (1 S 24)
- He did not wish evil to his son, Absalom, even though he turned against him. (2 S 19:1)
- He was humiliated and cursed by Shimei (2 S 16:5-24), but did not punish him. (2 S 19:24)

Again, look at your family unity, security in life and social status. Were there times when:

- You were tempted to put others down, to exclude them from your life?

- You had feelings of revenge and vindictiveness for wrong done to you?
- You were betrayed or cheated by a close friend or colleague?
- You were badly hurt by a family member?
- In your response to such situations, did you give in to your natural impulses or did you act, strengthened by God's love and wisdom?
- Take a moment and, as you relive some situations, allow Jesus to heal you, to strengthen you and love you.

Even though he was God-chosen and very successful, David was human and sinned. He gave in to his physical lust and sinned against Uriah and his wife, Bathsheba. (2 S 11) Yet, on Nathan's admonition, he accepted his sin, repented (2 S 12:7; Ps 51) and accepted God's justice.

Look at yourself and get in touch with your failures and sinfulness:

- Do you accept that, even though you are blessed, you are also a sinner?
- How do you deal with sin in your life?
- Do you keep fighting and denying your sinfulness, or do you humbly own it and turn to Jesus for forgiveness?
- How do you reconcile the fact that you are a "Loved Sinner"?
- Generally speaking, do you use all your energy:

  - To fight a couple of defects?
  - Or to strengthen and improve your virtues and giftedness?

Before you end the prayer, I invite you to join King David in thanking the Lord for all that He does for you. You can join David by lovingly reading 2 Samuel 22 or, if you want to be personal, compose your own song of gratitude to Jesus, your greatest and most intimate friend.

8.
JONATHAN

(1 Samuel 18-24; 2 Samuel 1)

WHEN Jonathan witnessed David's victory over Goliath, he was strongly attracted to David, loved him and desired a good friendship. "By the time David finished speaking with Saul, Jonathan had become as fond of David as if his life depended on him. He loved him as he loved himself. . . . And Jonathan entered into a bond with David, because he loved him as himself." (1 S 18:1, 3)

Think of your best friend and become aware of the marvelous gift of friendship:

- Who is your best friend?
- Where and how did you meet?
- What attracted you to each other?
- Were you moved to love your friend or were you asked into this friendship?
- Was your love certain, sincere and strong from the beginning?
- How was your friend affected by your love or what effect did your friend's love have on you?

Jonathan loved David "as he loved himself." "Jonathan divested himself of the mantle he was wearing and gave it to David, along with his military dress and his sword, his bow and his belt." (1 S 18:4)

As you reflect on your love for your best friend:

- Can you say that you love your friend as you love yourself?
- How strong and deep is the bond of friendship between you?
- What does your friendship cost you?
- Is your love for your friend unconditional like Jonathan's?

Jonathan's unconditional and enduring love for David meant protection and justice. Because Jonathan loved David as himself, he protected him by informing him of Saul's intent to kill him: "My father Saul is trying to kill you . . . get out of sight and remain in hiding. . . . If I learn anything I will let you know" (1 S 19:2-3) and by trying to convince his father not to kill David. (19:4-7)

As you admire Jonathan's sincerity in protecting David, look at your love and friendship:

- Were there times when your friendship was threatened because of jealousy, envy or bad feelings from other friends?
- Which side did you take as you faced such threats?
- What priority did you give to your friend as you defended and protected her/him?
- Or did you ignore the friendship and become self-centered and fearful?
- Like Jonathan, are you ready to risk your life for the sake of your friend?
- How does Jesus come into your life right now?

Friendship and love have their low moments. In such moments, Jonathan proved himself a consoler and encourager.

"Go in peace, in keeping with what we two have sworn by the name of the Lord. The Lord shall be between you and me and between your posterity and mine forever." (1 S 20:42)

"Have no fear, my father Saul shall not lay a hand on you. You shall be king of Israel and I shall be second to you." (1 S 23:17)

Become aware of your friend's history, especially moments of loss, failure or tragedy:

- Have you always been the first to be at your friend's side at such times?

- What qualities and virtues did you share with your friend in times of need?
- Were your consolation and encouragement in word and/or in deed?
- Did your friend's pain become your own because of the strong bond between you?
- In your honest care and love, are you patient and soothing or nervous and irritable?

When Jonathan died, David honored him with deep-felt affection:

"I grieve for you, Jonathan, my brother! Most dear have you been to me; more precious have I held love for you than love for women." (2 S 1:26)

Before you end your prayer, imagine you have lost your friend and, as you experience the loss, join David in honoring your friend with your sincerest feelings:

- Do you see in your friend a real brother or sister?
- Can you truly say of your friend: "Most dear you are to me"?
- Do you hold your friend more precious than anyone else?

As you get in touch with the rich qualities of your friendship, thank Jesus for the qualities you possess and, if you feel like it, call or write to your friend and express your present love and appreciation.

9.
ISAIAH

(Isaiah 6)

ISAIAH is the greatest prophet who was called by God at a critical moment in Israel's history. I invite you to join this prophet in experiencing his call and mission and to be generous with him in his response and struggle.

Because his mission was great and demanding, Isaiah was called in a special way as he saw God's glory and heard the seraphim sing His praises.   (Is 6:1-2)

Imagine yourself in the church you frequent most. Become aware of the altar where Jesus is enthroned, feel the holiness of the place where you are seated and go back to the time when YOU experienced God's glory as He called you to your mission in life:

- Where were you when Jesus called you?
- In what way have you experienced God's glory and power?
- Was this glory majestic and transcendent?
- Or simple and ordinary yet deeply felt, in the stillness of your being?

Isaiah's reaction to God's presence was an awareness of his sinfulness. "Woe is me, I am doomed! For I am a man of unclean lips, living among a people of unclean lips."   (Is 6:5)

- What reactions did you feel?
- Were you surprised, excited, joyful, alarmed?
- Has the Lord's brightness brought you in touch with the dark shadow of your sinfulness and inadequacy?
- How was Isaiah's reaction reflected in yours?
- Take some time and relive these feelings as you experience God's first call to you.

Because Isaiah was honest and humble, he was purified to meet God and listen to His message. "One of the seraphim . . . holding an ember . . . touched my mouth with it. 'See,' he said, 'now that this has touched your lips, your wickedness is removed, your sin purged.' "   (Is 6:6-7)

When you experienced God's glorious presence and felt your limitations:

- Did you run away from the Lord in ignorance or fear?
- Or did you prostrate yourself before Him, allowing Him to purify you?
- From what fears, inadequacies, sins and anxieties did the Lord cleanse you?
- Who was the agent of this purification for you?
- Was it easy or hard for you to admit your limitations and allow God's agent to purify and strengthen you?

Purification led Isaiah to open himself to God and to answer promptly and generously.

" 'Whom shall I send? Who will go for us?' 'Here I am,' I said, 'send me.' " (Is 6:8)

Recall your calls in life:

- Have you always been prompt and generous in saying "yes" to the Lord?
- In difficult situations, what made it hard for you to say "yes" to Jesus?
- Was it self-love, love for other people, attachment to a belief or attitude?
- When and how did purification happen in you that led you to say "yes"?
- Take a moment of prayerful reflection and let your heart open itself into the heart of Jesus.

When Isaiah offered himself to the Lord, he was given a very hard mission to fulfill, a mission that brought worry and anxiety. (Is 6:11-13)

"You are to make the heart of this people sluggish, to dull their ears and close their eyes . . . else . . . they will turn and be healed." (6:10)

Throughout his mission, Isaiah was faced with the moral breakdown of Judah and Jerusalem. He faced kings and pleaded with them to keep and renew their faith in the living God and he denounced very strongly the ''covenant with death'' that Hezekiah made with Egypt. (Is 30-31)   Again and again Isaiah denounced sins, preached destruction, offered hope to the faithful remnant (Is 24)   and foretold salvation and redemption (Is 28, 29, 35, 43)   through the Emmanuel oracles   (Is 7)   and the Suffering Servant songs. (Is 49-53)

As you reflect on the variety of approaches that Isaiah used to fulfill his mission and how God was always the source and backbone of his strength and success, get in touch with your own mission in life:

- What missions has Jesus entrusted to you in life?
- Are these missions at home, at work, in the community, in modern society?
- What conflicts do you face in your mission: addictions, unbelief, materialism, licentiousness, generation gaps, opposite attitudes in the church?

Take these conflicts one by one and see:

- How does each conflict affect you?
- How do you react to each conflict?
- What strength or quality do you use in facing each problem?
- What weaknesses cause your struggle to fulfill your mission?
- When struggles and confrontations arise, how do you face them?
- In your mission, are you always a prophet of doom, denouncing evil?
- Or do you offer hope of redemption and salvation?
- How often, like Isaiah, do you foresee and foretell:

  - A renewal of the modern Israel? (Is 61, 62, 66)
  - The glory of the modern Zion? (Is 60, 65)

Before you end this exercise, take a few moments and become aware of some special touch of the Lord during this prayer-period and:

- Thank Jesus for calling you and giving you your mission.
- Thank Him for the way you have handled your mission till now.
- Ask Him to strengthen you, to deepen your hope and broaden your trust so that with Isaiah you will be able to proclaim: "All who see them shall acknowledge them as a race the Lord has blessed." (Is 61:9)

You may end the prayer by praying Isaiah 60.

10.
JEREMIAH

(Jeremiah 1:4-10)

I INVITE you to spend some time with Jeremiah as God calls him, and to let the circumstances of his call touch your heart as YOU experience Jesus calling you in your life.

"Before I formed you in the womb, I knew you." (Jr 1:5) This is how God introduced Himself to Jeremiah. God chose Jeremiah and wanted him to live. Look at yourself, at the circumstances of your birth and the family into which you were born:

- Do these facts tell you that God KNEW YOU even before your parents conceived you?
- Today, what signs, proofs and affirmations do you have that God chose you and desired you to live?

- Are you pleased with God's choice and desire of sharing life with you?
- What feelings and responses do you experience as you are alive and known by God?

"Before you were born, I consecrated you." (Jr 1:5)   God consecrated Jeremiah for Himself. Consecration means "being set apart from a worldly mentality and attached to the mentality of Jesus." As you look at your personality:

- Name the virtues, qualities and spiritual gifts you possess.
- What natural talents and skills do you have?
- How have your family, your society and your education helped you to be the mature person you are?

Look at who you are today and your ambitions in life. Become aware of your behavior and dealings with others:

- In all that you say and do, do you try to put on the attitude of Jesus?
- Are you interested in and do you use your giftedness to enhance God's glory and praise?
- Or do you crave self-pride, self-satisfaction and a good name?
- Can you sincerely say that you are attuned to the heart and mind of Jesus? (cf. the Beatitudes, Matthew 5)

"I have appointed you a prophet to the nations . . . you shall go to whomever I send you; you shall speak whatever I command you." (Jr 1:5, 7)   A prophet is one who speaks in the name of God. In your own way and according to your mission in life, YOU TOO are a prophet because you are baptized in the name of the Triune God.

I invite you to go back into your life-history and, as you get in touch with the main stepping stones and decisions in your life:

- Name those stepping stones or decisions which you feel Jesus used to prepare you for your present mission.
- What events, talents, successes and rejections in life tell you that Jesus has not only chosen you to live but also appointed you to share His saving mission?
- Where and to whom do you feel sent? And what is your mission?
- What have you to offer in deed, word or in silence to those people to whom Jesus sent you to minister?

Take a few moments and recognize the dignity and responsibility you have as you consider the choice of Jesus to share His life and mission with you. Spend some time in silent gratitude, praise and glory to your Creator and Lord.

Jeremiah KNEW how much God loved him and he soon became aware of his human limitations. In real fear and unworthiness, he protested: "Lord God, I do not know how to speak, I am too young." (Jr 1:6)

I invite you to look at your present ministry in life, be it in the family, in a community or at work. You know very well that you are abundantly blessed and personally loved by God, yet there are many times in life when you are afraid, insecure, doubtful — and this freezes and paralyzes you:

- What people, challenges and risks make you say: "I am too young, inexperienced"?
- What people, circumstances and events make you whisper: "I do not know how to talk"?
- In front of whom or what, do you feel unworthy, not trained, insecure and helpless?
- Do you allow such inferiority feelings and insecure emotions to freeze and paralyze you as if everything depends on you?

- Or do you use your spiritual powerhouse by seeking light, courage and wisdom from Jesus?
- Take some time and, as you become aware of fears, insecurities and inferiorities:

    - Offer them to Jesus.
    - Ask Him to purify you from your pride and self-trust.
    - And let Him empower you with His grace as you hear Him telling you: "Do not say, 'I am too young!' . . . have no fear . . . because I am with you to deliver you." (Jr 1:7-8)

Take a few moments and, when you are ready, end the exercise.

11.

HANNAH

(1 Samuel 1)

IN THE FIRST BOOK of Samuel we read of Elkanah, a God-fearing man who had two wives. Peninnah was the mother of many children while Hannah was barren. In your prayer, I invite you to spend time with Hannah and learn from her as you befriend her.

Get in touch with Hannah's feelings as a barren woman living with Peninnah, the mother of a big family. Observe Peninnah's behavior, listen to her remarks and see her despising Hannah because of her barrenness.

Now look at yourself in your family or at work:

- How do the members of your family or your co-workers look at you and treat you?
- Do they know of any of your serious defects?

- Who, in your family or at work, makes sport of you, uses you as a laughingstock and ridicules you for your defects?
- How much and where does it pain you to be frequently reminded of your defects?
- How do you deal with your feelings?
- Do you just weep silently and refuse to eat (1 S 1:7) or do you get angry, become violent and hurt back?
- What is YOUR response to the people who hurt you?

Hannah's response to Peninnah's humiliations was an outpouring of her sorrow to the Lord: "In her bitterness she prayed to the Lord, weeping copiously." (1 S 1:10)

In imagination, go back to the past and reflect on the people who hurt you, on humiliations received or events which wounded you deeply. As you look at these painful moments:

- Was your reaction one of bitterness, anger and revenge or was it one of humility and dependence on God?
- Were your feelings those of pardon and understanding or vindictiveness and revenge?
- In such circumstances, did you turn to the Lord for enlightenment and inspiration or did you turn against God?
- Did you have anyone with whom you could share your humiliations, hurts and anger?
- How has this friend led you to acceptance, understanding and a change of heart?

Hannah was not angry at God. In her pain and sorrow she prayed honestly and she asked for what she really wanted: "If you give your handmaid a male child, I will give him to the Lord for as long as he lives; neither wine nor liquor shall he drink, and no razor shall ever touch his head." (1 S 1:11)

I invite you to look at your prayer life. From experience, what discernment do you make:

- Does your prayer life suffer because of negative events?
- Do negative events divert your intentions and attitudes in prayer?
- In such times, do you stand by what you really want to pray for, or does your heart concentrate on those things for which, in fact, you do not really want to pray?

Hannah wanted a male child. She asked for him with deep faith and trust, and she even promised that if God were to hear her, she would consecrate her child to the Lord's service. In your prayer:

- Do you always know those things for which you are praying?
- Are you aware of the consequences of God hearing your prayer?
- Are you ready, like Hannah, to offer back to God what is offered you in response to your prayer?
- How honest and sincere is your prayer? ". . . I am an unhappy woman . . . my prayer has been prompted by my deep sorrow." (1 S 1:15-16)
- How faith-filled, selfless and Christ-oriented is your prayer?

Because of her honesty, sincerity and selflessness, Hannah's prayer was heard. "She conceived . . . and bore a son whom she called Samuel." (1 S 1:21) Hannah kept her promise and "once he was weaned, she brought him up with her . . . and presented him at the temple of the Lord." (1:24) She said to Eli, the priest: "Now I give him to the Lord. As long as he lives, he shall be dedicated to the Lord." (1:28)

Before you end your prayer, get in touch with the times when your prayer was heard. In your joy and happiness:

- Did you quickly forget the past or did you return to give thanks to God?
- If you made any promises, did you, like Hannah, fulfill them willingly?

- Or were you so attached to the gifts received that you found it hard to keep your promise?

Take a few moments and, as you become aware of what is going on within you, turn toward Jesus and join Hannah in praising and thanking God either by praying 1 Samuel 2 or by saying your own Magnificat.

12.
JOB

(Job 1-7, 31)

AS YOU START your prayer, I invite you to identify yourself with Job.

Job is described as a ''sound and honest man who feared God and shunned evil . . . indeed a man of mark among all the people of the East.'' (Jb 1:1, 3)

Imagine that your best friend is asked to eulogize you at a dinner party:

- Who is this friend who knows you most?
- From all the knowledge your friend has of you, what do you hear being said about you?
- Do you listen calmly and take in all that you are eulogized for?
- Do you agree with all that is being said about you?
- What feelings and emotions arise within you as you see yourself admired by the guests?
- As you look around you, can you feel the attitude of some of the guests towards you?

- Take a few moments and thank Jesus for the affirmation you experience and for the confirmation of being ''a person of mark'' that the eulogy and the guests are offering you.

In the midst of a very happy family life blessed with children, hundreds of cattle, prosperity and feasting, Job was struck with disaster and misfortune so extensively that all prosperity and joy were taken away from him. His reaction to this calamity was: ''Naked I came from my mother's womb, naked I shall return. The Lord gave, the Lord has taken back. Blessed be the name of the Lord.'' (Jb 1:21)

As you become aware of Job's misfortune, I invite you to look back at your life and to allow your imagination to unfold to your memory and feelings, all the personal pains, hurts and rejections, material calamities, academic and social failures that make up the sorrowful mysteries of your life:

- Take your time and, as different painful catastrophes unfold to you, become aware of your reaction in feelings and behavior.
- As you look back at this negative aspect of your life, get in touch with the way you dealt with every disaster, however small it was.
- Was your reaction different from Job's?
- What made you react frightfully . . . angrily . . . thoughtlessly . . . or patiently and prudently?
- Do you see any faith or hope in your reaction, even though they were not always praiseworthy?
- If these misfortunes would happen again to you, do you think you would react differently to them now that you have grown spiritually?
- What about sickness or accidents that ruined your physical appearance?
- Can you say with Job, ''If we take happiness from God's hand, must we not take sorrow too?'' (Jb 2:10) or do you curse God for what happened to you every time you look in the mirror?

Experiencing your physical, spiritual and emotional tragedies, I invite you to kneel in front of the crucified Jesus and spend time with Him.

Let His unfailing love for you help you to unburden your pains, sadness and fears:

- "My only food is sighs, and my groans pour out like water." (Jb 3:24) Let your sighs rise from your heart and allow your painful and shameful groans to be poured into the heart of Jesus.
- "Whatever I fear comes true, whatever I dread befalls me." (Jb 3:25) Name your fears that come within you and are caused by exterior stimuli and, as you own them, ask Jesus to console and calm you.
- "For me, there is no calm, no peace, my torments banish rest." (Jb 3:26) What is it that makes your heart heavy, frightened and frozen? Feel it all, accept it and gently pass it on to Jesus to be purified and washed clean in His blood.

A characteristic of Job in his long struggle is his deep trust in God because he was convinced of his sincere holiness. (Jb 31) As you recognize your faith-filled relationship with Jesus take your time and, in all sincerity:

- Offer to Jesus all your hurts, anger, insecurity, uncertainty, anxiety.
- Quieten yourself and let Jesus answer you as He accepts your bleeding heart.
- Allow Job and mother Mary to be present at your dialogue and mutual sharing with Jesus.
- When you are ready, spend a few moments of silent adoration before Jesus crucified and feel Him coming down from the cross to hold you gently in His embrace as He tells you, "Come to me, you who labor and are burdened, and I will give you rest." (Mt 11:28)

13.

JONAH

(Jonah 1-4)

JONAH IS an image of the rebellious child in us, an image we often identify with as we face difficult challenges. For your prayer, I invite you to become Jonah and let his disobedience and bitterness become a part of you.

"The word of the Lord came to Jonah: 'Set out for the great city of Nineveh and preach against it.' " (Jon 1:1-2)

"But Jonah made ready to flee to Tarshish, away from the Lord. He went down to Joppa, found a ship . . . and went aboard to journey . . . away from the Lord." (Jn 1:3)

As you listen to God's voice within you, look at your past and become aware of some difficult calls you experienced in life:

- Where were you when God called you for such difficult actions?
- What self-image did you then have?
- In your opinion then, whom did God's mercy enfold?
- To whom did God send you?
- What made God's mission so hard for you that you bluntly disobeyed and ran away from Him?
- How and where did you flee from God's voice and mission?

God's calls are holy and His will comes true even though we put obstacles in His way. In the case of Jonah, God acted in an unusual way to let His will be done.

"Come, let us cast lots to find out on whose account we have met with this misfortune." (Jon 1:7)

"They took Jonah and threw him into the sea (Jon 1:15). . . But the Lord sent a large fish, that swallowed Jonah (2:1). . .

then the Lord commanded the fish to spew Jonah upon the shore.''
(2:11)

As you remember the ways you used to flee from the Lord:

- What means did you see to avoid fulfilling God's will?
- Who and what were the ship and the Tarshish you used?
- What storms arose within you (guilt, anxiety, conscience) that brought you in touch with your sinfulness and disobedience?
- Who and what were the fish of safety and survival for you?
- How and where do you see God's divine providence in this?
- What is happening within you now?
- Say something to Jesus as you are in the belly of the fish.

God's patience is indescribable when it comes to dealing with His chosen ones, especially when forgiveness is at stake. A second time God calls Jonah and commands him:

"Set out for the great city of Nineveh and announce to it the message that I will tell you." (Jon 3:2)

"Forty days more and Nineveh shall be destroyed." (3:4)

In spite of his resistance, Jonah accepted God's mission and faithfully fulfilled it.

Look at your life and become aware of the ways the Lord dealt with you to convince you that:

- You are His chosen instrument, however weak and sinful you may be.
- That you are chosen for a specific mission in life.

In spite of your human limitation and sinfulness:

- Are you convinced that Jesus chose you as His special instrument?
- What is the specific mission Jesus gave you in life?
- What do you like and dislike in your mission?

- What makes you obey God's will and undergo the implied hardships so faithfully?

The message of Jonah was so effective that, "When God saw by their actions how they turned from their evil way, He repented of the evil that He had threatened to do to them; He did not carry it out." (Jon 3:10)

Look at your life, enter into the goodness of your heart and become aware of times when, through your instrumentality:

- People turned away from sin and had a true change of heart.
- Someone was able to let go of anger and revenge and gave in to forgiveness.
- Someone felt peace, joy and love and consequently came nearer to Jesus.
- Someone was born to a new life in the Spirit.
- Thank Jesus for your instrumentality and for the many people who influenced you or whom you influenced.

When Jonah experienced the conversion of the Ninevites, he was angry at God's merciful love and he felt bitter because God did not destroy them. (Jon 4)   Like many of the Chosen People, Jonah was a victim to a narrow and vindictive mentality. He could not tolerate God's mercy over the wicked nations.

Before you end the exercise, take some time and consider:

- The ministry of other chosen instruments.
- Other people professing different beliefs.
- People of different race, color, culture, etc.
- Are you self-righteous, sure of salvation because you are a chosen instrument?

- Do you accept others or are you critical of the good they do?
- Are you cooperative with others for the growth of the Kingdom?
- Or do you want to control the whole show by yourself?
- Take a few moments of loving dialogue with Jesus and offer Him your failures and sinfulness. Ask Him to forgive you and to make you a better instrument in His hands.

14.
ELEAZAR

(2 Maccabees 6:18-31)

ANTIOCHUS, King of Syria, issued a decree to all Jews to abandon their customs and disobey the laws of God. Eleazar, a devout Jew, is an example of virtue and fidelity to God. He chose torment and death rather than abandon his God and religion.

In your prayer, get in touch with your faith and religion and with what they mean to you as a devout Christian:

- In what family and under what circumstances were you born?
- How did your parents live their faith and practice their religion?
- Who, besides your parents, introduced to you and deepened in you the conviction of faith and the practice of your religion?
- What people and events were influential in helping you build your deep faith?
- What value do you give to faith and religion?
- What are you doing to pass on your faith and religion to your family and friends?

Imagine the President issuing an order condemning your faith and religion, prohibiting you from practicing your faith both publicly and privately. This is what happened to Eleazar, a Jewish scribe who was noble and advanced in age. In such a case:

- Are you ready to obey the President? To oppose him or to compromise?
- Are faith and religion a matter of life and death for you or are they of secondary importance?
- Do you value human authority, honor and self-esteem more than God's law and love for you?
- How do you respond to human laws contradicting or opposing God's laws and your conscience?

"Eleazar preferred a glorious death to a life of defilement. He spat out the pork and went forward of his own accord to the instrument of torture." (2 M 6:19)

As you look at your life, become aware of events and times when you were challenged to choose between physical pleasure and inner peace of soul; between cheating, lying, hiding the whole truth and your self-integrity; between talking loudly and keeping silent. In these circumstances:

- What choices did you make?
- What convinced you to make such choices?
- Have you had to discern between wrong and right choices, selfishness and other-centeredness, self-satisfaction and God's love?
- Were your choices and conclusions always right?
- What were and are your feelings and convictions about: abortion, nuclear war, alcohol and drug abuse, prostitution, etc.
- Like Eleazar, are you ready to die in fidelity to your God, your faith and religion?
- How often are you not even aware of the problems existing next door to you or perhaps in your very house?
- As you become aware of your feelings, choices and responses, spend some time in loving dialogue with Jesus, the source of your life and faith.

The enemies of Eleazar tried to persuade him to cheat his own people by pretending to follow the king's order while eating meat that was lawful for him. (2 M 6:21-22) Yet Eleazar ". . . declared openly that above all he would be loyal to the holy laws given by God (6:23). . . . 'Therefore, by giving up my life now, . . . I will leave to the young a noble example of how to die willingly and generously for the revered and holy laws.' " (6:27-28)

Look at your faith journey:

- Are you actively witnessing your religion?
- Have you ever been confronted by others to deny, ridicule or unduly criticize your religion?
- How did you respond to such confrontations?
- Was friendship, human respect, self-esteem, peer pressure stronger than your affection for God and religion?
- Or was your faith so deep and your love for Jesus and His precepts so strong that, like Eleazar, you chose Jesus rather than let your faith be diminished and your religion ridiculed?

Eleazar offered his life to God and suffered martyrdom faithfully and lovingly: "Although I could have escaped death, I am not only enduring terrible pain in my body . . . but also suffering it with joy in my soul because of my devotion to Him." (2 M 6:30)

Before you end your prayer, take a few moments and become aware of your feelings and what is going on within you right now:

- In faith, allow Jesus to come to you and offer Him all that you have.
- In hope, ask Him to give you greater courage in the future to remain faithful to His precepts and guidance.
- In love, offer Him your whole self and ask Him to give you His love, in return, to strengthen you in living a virtuous life till the end.

15.
EZEKIEL

(Ezekiel 2-5, 33)

EZEKIEL IS APPOINTED by God as a watchman over Israel, sent to proclaim God's message to a rebellious people who would not listen.

Become aware of yourself as a modern parent, teacher, educator, employer or counselor. Be in touch with:

- Your gifts and skills in using these gifts.
- The people you are accountable for: Who are they? What background do they have?
- Your mission to these people and their general response to you.

Ezekiel is sent to a rebellious people (Ezk 2:3)   and is asked by God not to be afraid of their rejection and resistance (2:6) because they will refuse to listen to him. (3:7)

Become aware of people you associate with: family and friends, people with and for whom you work:

- Are these people as hard to deal with as Ezekiel's rebellious people?
- What made these people hard, resist challenges and afraid of risks?
- What helps you to persevere in keeping a good relationship with these people?
- Is it a sense of mission? Ambition and self-pride? A desire to see them healed?

Ezekiel's call came from above. "The spirit which had lifted me up seized me . . . while the hand of the Lord rested heavily upon me." (Ezk 3:14)

Go back to the time when you were called to your present ministry:

- Was your call just a human call, a yearning to use your gifts or skills?
- Or was it from above?
- What facts assure you that Jesus "lifted you up," "seized you" and "let his hand rest heavily upon you"?

"I have appointed you a watchman for the house of Israel." (Ezk 3:17)

- Are you convinced that God/Jesus appointed you to be the parent, teacher, leader that you are today?
- Become aware of the moment or event when you KNEW your appointment and accepted it.
- What does being a "watchperson" imply for you in your mission at home and at work?
- Who is your "Israel" over whom you are a watchperson?

Ezekiel was appointed watchman so that ". . . when you hear a word from my mouth, you shall warn them for me." (Ezk 3:17) Ezekiel fulfilled his responsibility by pointing out evil, danger and possible death (3:18-21) and by offering hope to the faithful remnant. (11:17-20, 16:53)

- At work, do you "watch over" others to help them grow or do you lead them to discouragement?
- What are your attitudes in pointing out weaknesses and correcting harm done?

- Do you take time to recognize growth, affirm positiveness and encourage weak yet willing people?
- Is your communication personal and warm or cold and impersonal?
- Do your attitudes and behavior show that you are a sensitive, loving and God-fearing person?

As a watchperson, Ezekiel had to watch carefully the behavior of the people and listen attentively to what God wanted him to proclaim to them. This careful watching and attentive listening meant painful discernment on the part of Ezekiel.

Look at your watching over, listening and discerning in life:

- Do you believe that you cannot build a community of love, peace and joy unless you discern every sign and action of the people for whom you are accountable?
- Is your discernment God-centered, self-centered or power and honor-centered?
- In reality, do you take time and pains to discern whether all that you see happening is:
  - Real or imaginary?
  - A projection of self or mirror of truth?
  - The result of personal conviction or of crowd pressure?
  - The result of human weakness or of an intrinsic evil will?

In communicating your messages to others:

- Are you certain that this is what God wants you to do?
- Are you truthful, honest and courageous?
- Or are you afraid, timid and tell people what they want to hear?
- Are you free from human respect, group pressure and the influence of "important" people?

Before you end the exercise, take a few moments of intimate prayer with the Lord:

- Thank Him for calling you to be a watchperson over your "house of Israel."
- Thank Him for the wisdom, sensitivity and discernment you possess that makes you a good watchperson.
- As you see yourself watching over, discerning what you see and hear and proclaiming your messages to others, ask the Lord to keep you near His heart so that your watchmanship will lead you to enter, together with your "house of Israel," into the glory of the temple of the Lord. (Ezk 43)

16.
THE IDEAL WIFE
(Proverbs 31:10-31)

IMAGINE this woman in front of you and, as you pray, become aware of your own identity. Praising this ideal woman, Lemuel writes: "When one finds a worthy wife, her value is far beyond pearls." (Pr 31:10) "Charm is deceptive and beauty fleeting; the woman who fears the Lord is to be praised." (31:30)

Looking at your lifestyle, do you feel that your spouse and others:

- Find in you a worthy person?
- What makes you worthy to your spouse, children and others?
- Do you consider yourself having a value beyond pearls?
- How and in what way do people value you?

- Do people value you for your passing charm and beauty or for the fear of the Lord that you show?

"She is clothed with strength and dignity, and she laughs at the days to come." (Pr 31:25)

- In what does your strength and dignity consist?
- Do you put your strength in physical health, financial wealth and material accumulation?
- Or do you place your dignity in honesty, self-sacrificing love and fear of the Lord?
- Have you ever placed your security in human respect, empty honor and riches that do not last?

The ideal woman/wife "opens her mouth in wisdom, and on her tongue is kindly counsel." (Pr 31:26)

Listen to your speech and the way you deal with people. Do people keep coming to you because:

- You have a wise heart and a prudent mind?
- In your presence, they always find spiritual and emotional uplifting?
- Through your words, they experience a refreshing and healing balm?
- What wisdom do you share with your family and others?
- What kindness do you show to those in need?

Wisdom shows itself in word and deed. The wise woman "reaches out her hands to the poor, and extends her arms to the needy." (Pr 31:20)

- Who are the poor and the needy with whom you come in contact?
- Do you extend your arms to the needy "out there" and close your heart to the crying "within your home"?

- What do you actually do as you stretch out your hand to the needy?
- Name the good you do, the help you offer, and the support you are.
- Bring to the Lord some of the "poor" and "needy" whom you enrich with your life.

The wise and compassionate woman is responsible. "She watches the conduct of her household." (Pr 31:27)

Observe yourself on an ordinary day:

- What do you do to watch the conduct of your family members?
- Do you impose yourself through preaching or do you invite by your examples?
- How do you fulfill your responsibilities of providing clothing (Pr 31:13) and food (31:15) for your family?
- In what ways do you use your health and strength (31:17) to build up a peaceful, happy and healthy family?
- What responses do you receive for your wise activity and compassionate guidance?
- Are you satisfied with the feedback you receive in word and deed?

Goodness and truthfulness are usually contagious and rewarding. The ideal woman is doubly recognized and honored.

"Her works praise her at the city gates" (Pr 31:31) and "her children rise up and praise her; her husband, too, extols her." (31:28)

Before you end your prayer, get in touch with the silence of your heart and:

- Look at your activity at home and at work and see what your behavior says about you.

- Listen to the praise and honor that your spouse and children give you and accept their grateful love for all that you are and give to them.
- Turn to Mary, the Mother of Jesus, and spend a few moments of loving dialogue with her.

17.

THE MACCABEAN MOTHER
(2 Maccabees 7)

"IT ALSO HAPPENED that seven brothers with their mother were arrested and tortured with whips and scourges by the king, to force them to eat pork in violation of God's law." (2 M 7:1)   "The mother was last to die, after her sons." (7:41)

In imagination, become present to the martyrdom of these seven children and their mother. Become aware of:

- The deep faith that this woman had and instilled in her children.
- The king's law ordering all Jews to violate God's law.
- The conviction of God's abiding presence and love that this family experienced.
- The great courage both children and mother showed in suffering torture and death to remain faithful to God's law.
- The effect all this should have had on the king, the torturers and on yourself.

As you pray this scriptural passage, I invite you to draw your attention to the mother who is the source of faith, fidelity and courage to herself and her seven children. Look at this wonderful example of a virtuous woman.

As she sees each of her children being tested, tortured and killed:

- Become aware of her feelings of love, compassion, tenderness and encouragement toward her children.
- Recognize the excellent training she gave to her children. She was determined and ready to sacrifice their lives because God had the first place in her heart and in the heart of her children.
- Realize that all this richness, beauty, glory and honor are present in her because of her deep faith and unshakable love for her God.

Now that you have experienced some of the strength and beauty of this Maccabean woman, I invite you to look at yourself. Realize that, like this woman, you, too, are created out of God's love. Likewise, you are blessed with faith and religion, intelligence and will, and enriched with love and discernment. As you recognize and accept your graces and blessings, talents, skills and other gifts:

- Are you fully aware of how precious, loved, blessed, honored and cared for you are by your Creator?
- In all honesty and truthfulness, do you accept all this positiveness?
- Or are you always complaining, comparing yourself with others, placing greater value on what and who others are and have, and not on what you truly are and have?
- How have you passed some of your richness to your children, relatives or friends?
- Do your behavior and attitudes confirm that you appreciate God and His gifts to you?
- What proofs do you have of living and sharing God's love for you as you look at your children, relatives and friends?

The deep faith and virtuous life of the Maccabean woman helped her to witness the martyrdom of her seven children and to endure her own death as a crowning of her family's faithfulness and loyalty to God. Her faith in the afterlife urged her to persuade and encourage her children to suffer such painful tortures.

Look at your faith-life and the vitality of your active spirituality. As you live your beliefs and practice your religion:

- How do you face the difficulties and problems of life?
- Is there any pain, evil, sickness or catastrophe that is too much for you?
- In times of trial and confusion, contradiction or rejection, where do you first turn your heart?
- When spiritual and material affliction hits you or your family, how are you helped by your faith in God and your spiritual richness?
- What does experience teach you as you look at your response to calamities and evil inclinations?
- How deep is your faith in the Resurrection and the afterlife?
- Do you have any experiences where your faith in the Resurrection influenced your choices and decisions?

Before you end the prayer, turn to Jesus, the Source of your faith:

- Thank Him for the faith with which you are blessed and for the many ways that your faith helps you to carry your crosses, to deny evil and to remain faithful to His guidance.
- Ask Him to give you a deeper share of the faith, love and virtue that the Maccabean woman had so that you, too, helped by grace, will be able to continue your faith-journey faithfully and successfully.

NEW TESTAMENT PATTERNS

18.

JOHN THE BAPTIST

(Luke 1, 3, 7; John 1, 3)

JOHN THE BAPTIST is an example of a contented person because he accepted himself as he really was. Being secure and fulfilled, he completed his mission generously till the end. As you reflect on John's life, I invite you to get in touch with the way you accept yourself and with the freedom with which you fulfill your mission in life.

"Do not be frightened, Zechariah; your prayer has been heard. Your wife Elizabeth shall bear a son whom you shall name John . . . he will be great in the eyes of the Lord . . . he will be filled with the Holy Spirit from his mother's womb." (Lk 1:13, 15) "Elizabeth gave birth to a son . . . and Zechariah wrote, 'His name is John.' " (Lk 1:57, 63)

As you listen to the circumstances of John's birth, I invite you to let your imagination unfold to you the circumstances of your own birth and name and become aware of feelings that arise in you:

- Who were your parents when you were born: their age, beliefs, financial security, etc.?
- Do you know the circumstances and time of your birth? Was there anything special about it?
- Do you like your name? What does it mean to you? How does it fit your personality?

- What made your parents give you your name?
- Spend a few moments talking to Jesus about your birth and name.
- Is there something special you want to share with Jesus that perhaps you are afraid to share?
- Allow Him to resolve your fears, and be truly honest about your feelings with Jesus.

John the Baptist's identity is clearly expressed by the evangelist. "There was a man named John sent by God, who came as a witness to testify to the light, so that through him all might believe." (Jn 1:6-7) As the Baptist grew, he knew exactly who he was and he openly professed, "I am not the Messiah, I am sent before Him . . . He must increase, while I must decrease." (Jn 3:28-30)

The Baptist was a contented person because he knew and accepted his true self. Look at yourself and allow your true identity to unfold itself to you as you get in touch with:

- What are your strengths and weaknesses, virtues and defects, creativity and limitations?
- Do you accept fully every aspect of yourself or do you keep comparing yourself with others?
- Are you a secure, happy and comparatively free person?
- Or do you feel inferior, insecure and unhappy, always desiring to be what others are?
- What witness do your body language, speech and attitudes give to others about yourself?
- Recognize the Baptist's transparent honesty and learn from him the secret of living your truthful and honest identity.

Zechariah foretold the Baptist's double mission in his song of praise: "And you, O child, shall . . . go before the Lord to prepare straight paths for Him, giving His people a knowledge of salvation in freedom from their sins." (Lk 1:76-77)

As the Baptist grew, he pointed to Jesus: "Look! There is the Lamb of God who takes away the sin of the world." (Jn 1:29) He also preached salvation through repentance from sin. John realized that the more faithful he was to his mission, the more would Jesus be made known and the less important he himself would become.

Take a few moments and try to experience yourself living your daily Christian life. Like John the Baptist, you, too, can make Jesus known to others and you can bring peace, life and salvation to them. Looking at your daily Christian life:

- Where, when and how do you feel an urge to bring Jesus to others?
- What people make you aware of the gift of Jesus in your life?
- What circumstances cause you to encourage people to discover and accept Jesus in their life?
- Do you talk freely about Jesus to others, or are you afraid to show you are a follower of Jesus?
- How do your lifestyle and behavior preach to others "salvation through a change of heart"?
- Does your life bear fruits that befit repentance like:

  - Sharing your possessions with others?
  - No cheating or bribery of any sort?
  - Being just and honest to all? (Lk 3:10-14)

- What price are you paying for your faithful witnessing to Jesus?
- Is it pain, suffering, humiliation, patience, abandonment, forgiveness?
- Can you sincerely say with John that through your daily witnessing, Christ is increasing and you are decreasing?

Throughout his life, John the Baptist gave light to those who sat in darkness and, by his death, he gave final witness to the Truth. (Mt 14:1-12) Because of such fidelity, Jesus praised John as a prophet "and something more . . . there is no man born of woman greater than John." (Lk 7:26-28)

In imagination, place yourself at the moment of your death. Look at your life experiences and, as you relive your love for Jesus and your witnessing to Him in your family, community and ministry, spend a few moments of silence and:

- Listen to what Jesus has to tell you as He approves and confirms you in what you are doing.
- Accept His strengthening grace.
- Ask Him to heal you and to help you persevere in your loving witnessing.
- As you gently end the exercise, thank Jesus for the person He made you to be and for the mission He shares with you. Ask Him to keep you close to His heart till you die in and for Him in peace and love.

19.
MARY, OUR LADY
(Luke 1-2)

I INVITE you to become present at Mary's call to be God's mother and to become aware of your main call in life.

"Rejoice, O highly favored daughter, the Lord is with you. Blessed are you among women." (Lk 1:28)

Mary, a teen-aged woman, is asked to rejoice because God has found favor in her and has chosen to be with her in a special way. As you reflect on this greeting to Mary, I invite you to go back to your early adolescence:

- When was the first time you remember being greeted or addressed by someone?
- Who was this person? Did this person represent someone else, a group or was the greeting given on their own behalf?
- What kind of greeting did you get?
- What feelings did you experience at this greeting: fear, joy, anxiety, exhilaration?
- Who were you then: your beliefs, health, philosophy, attitude toward life?
- How did you react to this person's greeting as you understood the content of the greeting?

"Mary was deeply troubled by his words and wondered what his greeting meant." (Lk 1:29)

According to her capability, Mary understood that something very special was happening to her. She also knew she was young and inexperienced. As you reflect on your main call in life and the stages of its unfolding, take a few moments and become aware of:

- What were the first signs you received about your call?
- Were these signs a strong feeling, a conviction, a person talking to you?
- As you were quite convinced of this special call, how did your inner self react to it?
- Did your mind wonder? Was your heart troubled? Did your body reject or accept it?
- Did this call fit your personality traits and academic training?
- Take some time and relive the event and the feelings you then expressed as Jesus was leading you to your mission in life.

Being human and limited, Mary was surprised at the great mission offered her. She doubted, and was not sure how God's desire would be realized through her. She was perplexed about becoming the mother of the God-child. In her wonder and surprise, she reflected (took time to be alone) and asked: ''How can this be since I do not know man?'' (Lk 1:34)

Again I invite you to remember your main call in life and also other important decisions you have made. In your response to the Lord's call for you:

- Do you take time to reflect on what is happening within you?
- Do you take time to pray about the means you have and how you can use them to give your best response?
- Do you ever think what the fruit of your decision and response will be?
- Do you realize that each response and decision is to be taken with God who invites you?

If all this is a reality in your life:

- If you doubt your goodness, is it because you need time and space to respond and decide?
- Why do you feel insecure and lack trust in God and confidence in your instincts and feelings?
- Take a few moments and share your feelings and thoughts with Jesus. Let Him respond to you as you offer Him all that is in your heart.

''And Mary said, 'I am the servant of the Lord. Let it be done to me as you say.' '' (Lk 1:38)

When Mary clarified her doubts, she accepted the Lord's call and opened her heart to all that the call could entail. As you reflect on your responses to God's calls to you, and as you become aware of decisions you made in life:

- Do you feel you have been fully generous and grateful to God in your response?
- Do you see yourself open-hearted as Mary was, or do you take over and respond as you want to?

- In living your calls and decisions, are you satisfied and pleased or do you need more adaptability and flexibility to let go of your fixations and let God's ways be acted in you?

Mary's response was not an isolated one. She kept listening and reflecting. The Gospel repeats that: "Mary treasured all these things and reflected on them in her heart." (Lk 2:19, 51)

This continual openness to God's call was painful and demanding yet it was so fruitful that Mary became "full of grace," "blessed among women," so that she could say, "All ages to come shall call me blessed." (Lk 1:28, 48)

As you look into your life:

- Do you, from time to time, provide space for yourself to check who, what and where you are?
- Do you ever stop DOING and start BEING?
- Are you willing to suffer the pain of not producing so as to gain awareness of your being?

Before you end this exercise, take a few moments to get in touch with what happened within you. As you renew your "Let it be done to me as you say" ask Jesus to give you the fullness of His grace and an abundance of His blessing.

20.
JOSEPH
(Matthew 1:18-25, 2:19-23)

ST. JOSEPH is an admirable person because of the great mission he so wonderfully and unobtrusively fulfilled as Mary's "husband, an upright man unwilling to expose her to the law, [who] decided to divorce her quietly.'' (Mt 1:19)

Joseph, A God-Fearing and Faith-Filled Person

"Joseph, son of David, have no fear about taking Mary as your wife. It is by the Holy Spirit that she has conceived this child.'' (Mt 1:20)

As you pray, I invite you to become Joseph and experience the problem with which he was faced. Joseph was anxious, suspicious of Mary, hurt and confused. Because he feared God, he believed the angel and agreed to wed Mary.

Reflect on your life and get in touch with problems, embarrassing experiences and painful decisions you faced in life. As you relive these realities:

- Realize the nature of these experiences.
- In what way were they painful, embarrassing, hurting?
- How did they affect your life and that of your family/community?
- Remember that faith and reverence helped Joseph accept what was naturally difficult to do.

"When Joseph awoke, he did as the angel of the Lord had directed him and received her into his home as his wife.'' (Mt 1:24)

- What made you accept your problems and decide on your way of action?
- Are you satisfied with what you have done?
- Were your decisions healthy, right and fruitful?

"She is to have a son and you are to name Him Jesus because He will save His people from their sins.'' (Mt 1:21)

Joseph had not only to accept Mary as his wife, he was also directed to name the baby when He is born. Because of his great faith and trust, Joseph was able to be responsible and obedient to God's will. His YES to God opened him to greater generosity as he had to respond to other calls.

As you reflect on some decisions you made in life:

- Do you see them as conclusive events or were they the beginning of a chain of other calls and responses?
- Were you always faithful and generous in your subsequent responses?
- What helped you to remain faithful in your smaller decisions and responses?
- Thank Jesus for all the qualities you possess that helped you to be faithful and generous in your responses.

Joseph, Protector and Guardian of Jesus and Mary

''The angel of the Lord suddenly appeared in a dream to Joseph with the command, 'Get up, take the child and His mother and flee to Egypt . . . Herod is searching for the child to destroy Him.' '' (Mt 2:13)

At times, God's ways are direct and demand immediate response. Again Joseph's fidelity is challenged, this time to be the protector of the holy family.

As you experience the insecurity, fear and trepidation of Joseph in accepting the message and passing it on to Mary, get in touch with similar situations in your life when you felt it hard to fulfill a difficult responsibility:

- What obstacles did you experience in these situations?
- To whom or to what did you turn for help and encouragement?
- What helped you guard or protect yourself and others?
- How was Jesus present in these events and active in you?

Because Joseph loved God and his family, he "got up and took the child and His mother and left that night for Egypt." (Mt 2:14)

- In circumstances similar to Joseph's, have you acted as promptly as he did?
- What made you act promptly even though you were inconvenienced?

Become consciously aware of your qualities and of how you have used them in different situations in life. Also let people who helped you act rightly come to your mind. As you name these blessings, be grateful to God, your Creator.

Joseph, A Loving and Silent Worker

Joseph built a healthy and happy family through his hard work. Because he loved much, he worked harder and better. In silence, he passed on many of his qualities to the child Jesus.

Look at yourself as a parent, teacher or guide:

- How do you see yourself passing on your qualities to those with whom you work?
- What feedback do you get from people with whom and for whom you work?
- In what ways is your working attitude similar or different from Joseph's?
- What can you do to grow in likeness to Joseph, the loving and silent worker?

Before you end the exercise, spend a few moments of intimate prayer with Joseph and ask him to intercede with Jesus for you as you work your way to become the person God wants you to be.

21.
PETER
(Matthew 16-17; Luke 5; John 1, 21)

I INVITE YOU to spend time looking at Peter and at yourself, and recognize similarities between you and Peter as Jesus calls you by name.

When Jesus met Peter for the first time, He LOOKED at him and, because He saw great potential in him, called him a ROCK. (Jn 1:42)

- Allow Jesus to meet you and look at you.
- What qualities, gifts and talents does Jesus see in you?
- As Jesus looks at your rich personality, what symbolic name would He give you?
- Listen to Jesus give you that name and see what it means to you.
- Knowing your family position and your mission in life, how does this name fit you?
- Do you like the name?
- What feelings does this name evoke in you: joy, surprise, fear, longing?
- Thank Jesus for recognizing your potential and affirming it by giving you the name. Offer Him your feelings as they arise within you.

As Peter grew in love and admiration for Jesus, the name ROCK helped him to grow from a self-centered security into a Jesus-centered faith. This was a painful and humiliating process. Yet because of sincerity, honesty and love, Peter became THE ROCK for the apostles and for the early Christian community.

I now invite you to get in touch with your Christian growth and allow Jesus to direct you into the fullest meaning of your symbolic name.

After teaching the crowds, Jesus asked Peter to throw the nets for a catch. Because of the circumstances, Peter told Jesus: "If you say so, I will lower the nets." (Lk 5:5) Being abundantly rewarded, Peter experienced mixed feelings. He knelt before Jesus lovingly and told Him, "Leave me, Lord, I am a sinful man." (Lk 5:8)

- In your life, when has Jesus asked you to say or do something you did not like, which did not seem fit or wise and, on doing it, you were greatly surprised at the fruitfulness of your action?
- What fears and anxieties did you experience as Jesus challenged you?
- When are you afraid to use strengths and gifts?
- What makes you avoid accepting your gifts and using them?
- At the same time, what draws you nearer to Jesus?
- Take some time in loving dialogue with Jesus as you share what is happening within you right now.

As Peter walked on the stormy water, he saw the wind, doubted and, in fear, called, "Lord, save me." Jesus told him, "Why did you falter?" (Mt 14:30-31)

- When you are overwhelmed with difficulties and problems, are you lost in your human limitations or do you seek and call Jesus?
- In loneliness and depression, in quarrels and disagreements, do you withdraw in self-pity or do you look ahead to catch hold of Jesus?
- How strong is your trust in Jesus' help?

- Do you go to Jesus by letting go of destructive loneliness and frustration?
- Offer all your weaknesses to Jesus and let Him call you to Him over the troubled waters of your life.

Like Peter, you are graciously blessed yet in need of healing and strength. As you look at your life, let meaningful events when Jesus affirmed you unfold themselves to you:

- What did you say or do that made Jesus affirm you with words like: "Blessed are you for you are a ROCK, a deep well, a high mountain . . ."?
- How affirmed, encouraged and strengthened did you feel as you experienced Jesus' love for you and trust in you? (cf. Mt 16:13-20)

In his spontaneity, Peter used the authority given him too quickly. As Jesus foretold His passion, Peter discouraged Him from accepting it because he was afraid. In return, Jesus calls Peter with another name: "Get behind me, Satan, you are thinking in human terms." (Mt 16:23)

- In what aspects of your life are you weak and vulnerable?
- Do you accept these weaknesses or do you refuse to acknowledge them because of other strengths you have?

In weaknesses and limitations, do you listen to Jesus as He tells you: "Get behind me, i.e., be my follower, be redeemed, take it slowly"?

In moments of success and growth, do you listen to the Father telling you: "Stop talking, here is My beloved Son, LISTEN to Him." (cf. Mt 17:5)

- What do successes and failures mean to you?
- Do you allow Jesus to touch your heart through them and help you feel His active presence in you?

After the triple betrayal, Jesus loved Peter all the more because the humiliation made Peter a wounded healer and a stronger rock. Jesus affirmed Peter in his rockness as a leader and joyfully accepted his purified love. (Jn 21:15-19)

As you look at yourself today, consider the process of your growth in spiritual freedom, in your positive approach to life and in your deeper intimacy with Jesus:

- What people, positive events and successes brought you to your spiritual growth?
- What humiliations, failures and sins made you aware of your fragile self still in need of healing and renewal?
- Who and what helped you let go of attachments to worldly honor and glory and convinced you of the strength that lies in depending on Jesus' loving compassion?

As you end this exercise, I invite you to spend a few moments in silent prayer and listen to the different times and ways that Jesus called you by name. Thank Him for all the ways that you have responded to Him and ask Him to continue leading you to a deeper and stronger intimacy with Him.

22.
THE BELOVED DISCIPLE
(John 1, 13, 19-21)

FOR YOUR PRAYER, accompany John, the beloved disciple, and with him, let Jesus love and befriend you.

A characteristic of John is his attraction to Jesus.

''The two disciples heard what he [John the Baptist] said, and followed Jesus.'' (Jn 1:37)

''Jesus . . . asked them, 'What are you looking for?' . . . So they . . . stayed with Him that day.'' (Jn 1:38-39)

In imagination go back to the time and place when you were first attracted to Jesus:

- Where were you? With whom? What was the occasion?
- Who or what pointed out Jesus to you?
- Look at Jesus as He presented Himself to you and take in all the details of His personality.
- What attracted you to Jesus?
- What did you say or do to show Jesus you were attracted to Him?

John stayed with Jesus and liked Him so much that, when afterward he was on the beach with his brother, James, and Jesus called them to become His followers, ''They abandoned their father, Zebedee . . . and went off in His company.'' (Mk 1:20)

Go back to your attraction to Jesus and the urge you felt to follow and befriend Him:

- How long did it take you to accept Him as your master and friend?
- In what ways did Jesus invite you to become His follower?
- What or whom did you have to abandon in order to ''go off'' with Jesus?
- Was this painful or was it an expected and joyful invitation?
- Reflect for a moment on the attraction that led you to follow Jesus.

John followed Jesus wholeheartedly. He wanted to know and love Him fully. He stayed with Jesus, listened to His wisdom, felt His care and compassion, experienced His forgiveness and took in His attitude so much that, after the Resurrection he could say: ''This is what we proclaim to you: What was from the beginning, what we have heard, what we have seen with our eyes, what we have looked upon and our hands have touched.'' (1 Jn 1:1)

As you reflect on your fellowship with Jesus over the years:

- Who and what led you to experience Jesus?
- Are there any special experiences in life when you truly saw, heard or touched Jesus?
- Can you honestly say that you KNOW Jesus because of your intimacy with Him?
- What part does prayer, self-abnegation and charity play in your personal experience of Jesus?
- How much do you relish your friendship with Jesus?
- Do you share His joy with those who hunger for the same love?

In the course of His ministry, Jesus had a special place in His heart for John:

- He gave John a glimpse of His future glory at His Transfiguration. (Mt 17:1-9)
- He allowed him to rest his head on His chest during the Last Supper. (Jn 13:23)
- He wanted him to witness the depth of His human weakness in the agony. (Mk 14:33)
- He entrusted him to His mother's care at the foot of the cross. (Jn 19:26)

As you reflect on these facts, become aware of the relationship of Jesus with you. You have followed Him sincerely even though, at times, you failed:

- Can you remember any special moments in life when Jesus showed you that you are special to Him?
- Are there any significant moments of prayer where Jesus touched you deeply?

- Is there any person in whom you experienced the personification of Jesus for you?
- Do you remember any special event, incident or happening where Jesus came face to face with you, unexpectedly yet forcefully?
- Take time to personalize these moments, people and events through which Jesus told you clearly: "You are special to me and I love you."

The predilection of Jesus for John resulted in John's delicate sensitivity to His presence and in his desire to remain with Him forever. After the Resurrection, it is John who:

- First peeps into the empty tomb. (Jn 20:5)
- Cried out at the miraculous catch of fish, "It is the Lord!" (Jn 21:7)
- Wrote down all that he witnessed in life and ". . . his testimony, we know, is true." (Jn 21:24)
- Accompanied Peter to the Temple, proclaimed the good news of Jesus there, and stood up to the Sanhedrin. (Ac 3:1-4:22)

Before you end this exercise, I invite you to get in touch with the growth of your respect and familiarity with Jesus. As you go through the process of growth, become aware of your intimacy with Jesus and:

- Relish your sensitivity to His presence in your life.
- Be grateful for your fidelity to prayer, intimacy and friendship with Him.
- Ask pardon for moments of weakness and selfishness.
- End your prayer rejoicing: "See what love the Father has bestowed on us in letting us be called children of God!" (1 Jn 3:1)

23.
MATTHEW

(Matthew 9:9-13)

I INVITE YOU to enter into the heart of Jesus as He calls Matthew to follow Him. Imagine Jesus walking along the road coming toward Matthew's office. As you accompany Jesus, stop in front of Matthew's office:

- Look at the office and see Matthew at his desk.
- Are there people in Matthew's office?
- Do you see other tax collectors?
- Are there people paying taxes or asking for a loan?
- What is Matthew saying and doing to these people?
- What feelings are you experiencing as you observe all this?
- Do you perceive any greediness or selfishness in Matthew?
- As you get in touch with your own feelings, become aware of your reactions to these feelings.

As you experience these feelings and pass your own judgments, Jesus enters the office. Like you, He observes Matthew and knows what kind of person he is. Jesus greets Matthew and with a determined voice tells him: ''I want you to be my follower.'' Without hesitation, Matthew stands up, leaves the office and follows Jesus.

- What are your feelings as all this happens in front of your eyes?
- Are you surprised, wondering if Jesus is sane and knows what He is doing? Or are you angry or perhaps jealous?
- Have you something to say or do to Jesus and do you have the courage to say or do it?

- Are your reactions to this invitation similar to or different from those of the other people present in the office?
- Look at Jesus and experience His feelings and thoughts as He sees Matthew responding promptly to His call.
- What are your feelings at Matthew's prompt and generous response?

Jesus knew that, as a tax collector, Matthew was greedy, selfish and, at times, misused his power. Still, He called him to be His follower. I invite you to look at your early adulthood:

- What kind of person were you then?
- What were your strengths and weaknesses?
- Did you ever misuse your strengths and gifts in school, at home or on the job to feel more secure, accepted and loved?
- Have your ever thought that Jesus knew exactly who you were then and what person you would become?

As you experience limitations and frustrations, become aware of the times and events in life when Jesus called you to follow Him:

- Where and when did Jesus call you?
- What people and circumstances did Jesus use to call you to Him and to put on His attitudes of love and compassion?
- Did the calls of Jesus come to you when you failed because you were weak or when you were proud and self-righteous?
- How did you respond to such invitations for growth and healing?
- Now that you are in touch with Jesus inviting you to be closer to Him, do you see any similarities between you and Matthew, between your relationship to Jesus and that of Matthew?

Matthew felt honored at Jesus' invitation. He showed gratitude to Jesus by sharing a dinner with Him and with other tax-collectors. Imagine yourself invited for this dinner:

- Do you accept the invitation or do you separate yourself from Matthew and his friends?
- Take some time and listen to what Matthew and some of his friends at the table are saying about themselves and about Jesus.
- Does anyone at the table say something to you? What have you to say?
- What feelings arise in you as you feel a part of this group?
- Look at Jesus and let Him talk to you, to Matthew and to the others. See what He has to say and let it go deeply into your heart.
- What have you to say to Jesus as you experience Him calling you to continue following Him?

At the criticism of the Pharisees, Jesus responded that "people who are well do not need a doctor" and that He came "to call sinners."

- Do you consider yourself socially and spiritually healthy or are you sick because of racism, sexism, or alcohol and drug abuse?
- When and how did you ever feel the need for Jesus to call you to HEALING AND FORGIVENESS?
- Do you resist Jesus because of pride and self-righteousness or because you are at rockbottom and do not feel worthy of His love?

Listen to Jesus telling you: "I have come to call sinners and outcasts." See him looking at you, inviting you to come closer to Him. In all truthfulness, thank Him for seeing the good in you, offer Him your sins and failures and ask Him to forgive you. As you experience His loving forgiveness and hear Him calling you to Him, go to Him wholeheartedly and tell Him: "Yes Lord, here I am, I come to do your will."

24.
THOMAS

(John 20:24-29)

THOMAS, the twin, is introduced by Mark (3:18): when Jesus "summoned the men He Himself had decided on . . . He named twelve as His companions whom He would send to preach the good news." (Mk 3:13-14)

When Jesus decided to go to hostile Judea, Thomas encouraged the other disciples, "Let us go along, to die with Him." (Jn 11:16)

During the last discourse of Jesus, Thomas asked Him, "Lord, we do not know where you are going. How can we know the way?" (Jn 14:5)

As you reflect on these statements, get in touch with the personality of Thomas:

- A courageous person with great potential for faithful companionship.
- A simple person, most probably a skilled farmer.
- An honest man, rather insecure and indecisive.
- A slow learner yet inquisitive for the Truth and seeking security.

I invite you to look at yourself and discover your qualities and limitations that made Jesus choose you to share His life and mission:

- What strengths do you share with Thomas?
- Do you feel any indecisiveness in action and decisions as Thomas did?

- Are you honest and humble enough to ask questions and clarify doubts in order to grow?
- Spend some time and let events and experiences show you similarities and differences from Thomas.

Thomas was faithful to Jesus because he trusted in Him and sincerely loved Him. As for you:

- What makes you seek and want to follow Jesus?
- What do you see in Jesus that attracts you to believe in and accept His way of life?
- In your weaknesses:

  - Are you humble and do you let Jesus guide you?
  - Or do you lack trust and want to be in full control?

- Spend a few moments with Thomas as you share your hidden feelings.

Thomas is widely known for his unbelief and cynicism in the Resurrection appearance. Recall Jesus appearing to the disciples and become the absent Thomas. As you join the disciples after the apparition and hear their story:

- Look at the other disciples and see what strikes you most in each of them.
- What feelings and emotions do these disciples express?
- Do you see any connection between their inner feelings and their exterior expression?
- What hinders you from accepting the experience of the disciples and from joining them in their joy and excitement?
- What makes you desire to touch and feel the wounds of Jesus to really believe:

  1) Is the obstacle coming from your personality, perhaps mistrust?

2) Is it hard-headedness, crass ignorance or a desire to be different?

3) Is it a sincere and honest quest because you are prudent, slow to act and desirous to have the whole truth?

Right now you may want to get in touch with personal experiences you have had and become consciously aware of your inner feelings as you discover similarities and differences in deed and speech between you and Thomas.

Gently become present to Jesus' second manifestation when He appeared to Thomas. Look at Jesus and listen to Him wishing you peace. Feel the silence in the room and see the joy on the faces of the other disciples.

Jesus knows your request, understands your unbelief and He asks you to go near Him and feel for yourself the wounds the nails have made:

- What are your feelings as Jesus adapts Himself to you and responds so gently to your request?
- Go to Him, look at His face, take His hands in yours and feel the wounds.
- What is going on in you as Jesus offers you this great privilege of being so close to Him?

Thomas' response to the Lord's gentle love was one of deep faith: "My Lord and my God!" What is YOUR reaction to Jesus responding to your needs and requests?

As you respond to the gentle love of Jesus for you, spend some time of intimate union with Him. Let Him show you where and how you need to grow and open your whole being to His laboring in you.

When you are ready, thank Jesus for the gift of faith and ask Him to keep you close to His heart till the end of your days.

25.
PAUL

(Acts 9:1-19)

As you reflect on Paul's call to follow Jesus, I invite you to become aware of the ways you are called to accept Jesus more fully in your life.

"Saul, still breathing murderous threats against the Lord's disciples, went to the high priest and asked him for letters which would empower him to arrest and bring to Jerusalem anyone he might find, man or woman, living according to the new way." (Ac 9:1-2)   Saul, a fanatical Jew full of hatred for the Christians, is met by Christ as he misuses his zeal and religious beliefs.

I invite you to become aware of your religious feelings towards your neighbor:

- How convinced are you of your faith and religious beliefs?
- In your religious zeal, whom do you willingly exclude from your love?
- What is your attitude toward blacks, gays, lesbians, the divorced, prostitutes and criminals, the economically poor?
- What are your feelings toward the more gifted and the poorer and handicapped members of your family and staff?
- How do you judge these people and what are your reactions to them?
- Do you accept them as God's chosen ones or do you withdraw from them and exclude them from your life?
- Take some time and become aware of similarities between you and Saul and get in touch with your feelings right now.

"As he . . . was approaching Damascus, a light from the sky suddenly flashed about him. He fell to the ground and at the same time heard a voice saying, 'Saul, Saul, why do you persecute me? . . . I am Jesus, the one you are persecuting.' '' (Ac 9:3-5)

In his religious fanaticism, Saul did not realize his sinfulness. But in reality he was persecuting Jesus because of his hatred for the Christians. Again I invite you to become aware of your interior attitudes and exterior behavior. As you become aware of people you exclude from your life and the feelings you bear for them, go deeper into your heart and recognize:

- What principles or convictions cause you to block these people from God's and your love?
- How did you come to hold so fast to such principles and convictions?
- As you delve into your conscience, do you see anything wrong with your attitudes and behavior?
- Have you ever experienced Jesus calling you by name and asking you why you are rejecting Him?
- What and who does Jesus use in your life to let you know that your attitudes and behavior are hurting you?

When Paul heard the voice of Jesus, he quickly responded by asking, ''Who are you, sir?'' and he humbly allowed himself to be led to Damascus and be baptized in the name of Jesus by Ananias. Paul became a fervent disciple of Jesus because he listened to the Truth and offered himself in His service humbly and generously.

Take a few moments and become aware of your responses to the various calls you receive to correct yourself, to change and to adapt:

- In your life, who is there that challenges you to be more open to Christ's mentality and attitude?
- What experiences make you realize that you are ready for renewal, better understanding and more participation in the Church?

- What events have you experienced that have taught you the need
  of a sincere forgiveness of the past and a gentle adaptation to the
  present in your family, in the Church and in society?
- Become aware of what is happening within you right now.

Imagine Jesus in front of you, He who gave you life and many
blessings, the faith you profess and the personality you possess:

- Open your heart fully to HIM and LET HIM talk to you.
- Listen to what He tells you and become aware of your feelings.
- Take time to be grateful for what is good within you.
- Ask pardon for your religious fanaticism, possessive attachment
  to tradition and lack of sensitivity for the less privileged. Open
  your heart for greater readiness to follow Jesus more generously
  and truthfully, in joys and in pain, as you hear Him telling you
  that you are "the instrument I have chosen to bring my name to
  the Gentiles and their kings and to the people of Israel."
  (Ac 9:15)

Take a few moments and, when you are ready, gently end the
exercise.

26.
MARTHA
(Luke 10:38-41; John 11-12)

ST. LUKE PRESENTS Martha as an extroverted woman who showed
her love for Jesus in word and deed, and St. John says of her that
"Jesus loved Martha and her sister and Lazarus very much."
(Jn 11:5)

During this prayer, I invite you to identify with Martha for a while and to draw fruit from your observations.

Martha's relationship with Jesus was very open and demonstrative, one of sincere sharing and loving service.

I invite you to imagine Jesus visiting your house and, during the visit, try to identify yourself with Martha. As Jesus rings the doorbell and you open the door for Him, let Him in and become aware of your feelings and behavior:

- What did you do to prepare yourself for Jesus' visit?
- Did you clean the house? Have you cooked something special for Him?
- Have you planned for His visit or did you want to let Jesus plan His visit?
- How do you welcome Jesus? What do you say and do for Him?
- How is Jesus responding to your welcome and hospitality?
- Are you alone in the house or are there other family members?
- Do you introduce them to Jesus or do you let them introduce themselves?
- Do you enjoy being with and listening to Jesus or do you feel the need of waiting on Him?
- Do you enjoy what you are doing for Jesus or are you distracted with the way others relate to Jesus?
- Are you comfortable with YOUR way of loving Jesus or do you feel like telling Him, "Lord, are you not concerned that my sister has left me to do the household tasks all alone?" (Lk 10:40)
- As you become aware of your relationship with Jesus, own it and accept it and thank Him for who you are and for the way He accepts you as you are.

Martha's prayer life was one of petition, expression and feeling. When Lazarus was seriously ill, Martha sent a quick and hope-filled message to Jesus, "Lord, the one you love is sick.'' (Jn 11:3)   A short petition, full of anxiety, eager to have Jesus respond at once.

Hence, when she heard that ''Jesus was coming, she went to meet Him.'' (Jn 11:20)

- In the different circumstances of life, do you feel the need of going to the Lord yourself?
- Is this urge to meet Jesus present only in painful and difficult events?
- Or is it also present in peaceful and joyful ones?
- What makes you want to meet Jesus? Curiosity and restlessness or love and companionship?

When Martha reached the place where Jesus was, she expressed impatience, impetuosity and some irritability. In all honesty, she told Him, ''Lord, if you had been here, my brother would never have died. Even now, I am sure that God will give you whatever you ask of Him.'' (Jn 11:21-22)

Martha unburdened her heart to Jesus freely and sincerely with many words and deep feeling, believing that He still could do something for Lazarus.

Being sensitive to Martha, Jesus comforts and consoles her with more words, ''I am the resurrection and the life . . . whoever is alive and believes in me will never die. Do you believe this?'' (Jn 11:25-26)

Martha is comforted and this deepens her faith in Jesus, ''Yes, Lord, I have come to believe that you are the Messiah, the Son of God: He who is come into the world.'' (Jn 11:27)

As you listen to Martha's conversation with Jesus, I invite you to become aware of your prayer style:

- Are you familiar with Martha's way of prayer?
- Do you feel comfortable talking to Jesus about your troubles, sorrows, pains and failures?

- Can you freely share with Jesus your anger, anxiety, irritation with Him, with others and with yourself?
- Or do you repress this honest and sincere sharing, pretending these feelings are not real?
- What do you learn from Martha's personality and prayer style?

Because Martha was honest with Jesus, she found healing, refuge and strength which she quickly shared with her sister. "She went back and called her sister Mary. 'The Teacher is here, asking for you,' she whispered." (Jn 11:28)

Prayer helped Martha to calm down, to deepen her faith in Jesus and to respect her sister's feelings. As you look at your prayer life:

- Do you feel that prayer helps you to grow in newness and freedom?
- Can you truly say that prayer affects your personality and your relationships with God and with others?
- In what ways does prayer offer you peace of soul and joy of heart?
- Thank Jesus for the fruit of your prayerfulness as He adapts to your personality.

Like Mary, Martha showed her gratitude to Jesus in deed. "Six days before Passover, Jesus came to Bethany. . . . There they gave Him a banquet, at which Martha served." (Jn 12:1-2)

Before you end this prayer, take a few moments and experience the deeply felt love of Jesus for you and, as you relive in imagination some meaningful events in your life:

- Become aware of the way you expressed your gratitude to Him.
- As you feel right now, renew your gratitude to Jesus.
- Thank Him for all His love for you and for the life-giving relationship you have with Him.
- When you are ready, gently end the exercise.

27.

MARY (MARTHA'S SISTER)
(Luke 10:38-41; John 11-12)

ST. LUKE PRESENTS Mary as an introverted and contemplative woman, and St. John says of her that "Jesus loved Martha and her sister and Lazarus very much." (Jn 11:5)

During this prayer, I invite you to identify with Mary and to draw fruit from your observations.

Mary's relationship with Jesus was one of listening, relishing and just being with Him that led her to a close, intimate union.

Imagine Jesus visiting you at home. He has a busy day, yet He passes by your house, and stops for a while to show that He cares:

- Listen to Jesus ringing the door bell or knocking at your door.
- What time of the day is it?
- Open the door and, as you recognize Jesus, become aware of your reactions.
- What are your first reactions as you see Jesus?

  - Are you embarrassed because the house is not fully clean?
  - Do you say something as you become conscious of the aroma of food being cooked?
  - Do you become conscious of your comfortable clothes and feel uneasy?
  - Or do you rejoice at the surprise that Jesus gives you and invite Him in?
  - What does Jesus tell you as you let Him in?
  - Does He sit down or does He make Himself comfortable and stay with you, asking you to finish what you are doing?

When Jesus visited Mary's house, Mary "seated herself at the Lord's feet and listened to His words." (Lk 10:39)

- What is YOUR way of welcoming and accepting Jesus?
- Do you stop whatever you are doing and give your full attention to Jesus?
- Or do you let Him feel at home and be with you and with what you are doing?
- What is YOUR way of listening to what Jesus has to tell you?
- Slow down for a few moments and listen to Jesus. Take in all that He says and does for you.
- As you listen to Jesus, can you sincerely hear Him telling you, "You have chosen the better portion and you shall not be deprived of it"? (cf. Lk 10:42)
- Spend a few moments in gratitude for Jesus' love for you and for your response to His relationship.

Mary's prayer life was one of listening, contemplating and feeling. When Lazarus was seriously ill, Mary sent a deep-felt message to Jesus, "Lord, the one you love is sick." (Jn 11:3)   A short, yet very emotional message.

Mary's love for Jesus developed into a very deep faith in Him. She felt that Jesus would surely do something for her brother. Because of this deep faith, "when Martha heard that Jesus was coming she went to meet Him, while Mary sat at home." (Jn 11:20)

- In your prayer time, in times of difficulty and when things go wrong, do you become emotional and turn the world upside down?
- Or do you "sit at home" waiting hopefully for the Lord to act?
- Is your prayer one of trust, abandonment and hope, or is it filled with worry, helplessness and feeling at a loss?

When Martha told Mary that the Lord is asking for her, ''she got up and started out in His direction.'' (Jn 11:29)   Even though sorrowful and grieving over the loss of Lazarus, Mary responds to Jesus and seeks comfort and consolation in Him.

''When Mary came to the place where Jesus was, seeing Him, she fell at His feet and said to Him, 'Lord, if you had been here my brother would never have died.' '' (Jn 11:32)

- Mary expressed deep emotions: She looks at Jesus, falls in adoration at His feet, weeps because she lost her brother, and her few words are filled with deep sorrow.
- Mary is emotional, full of feeling, a woman of a few words. Her prayer is less verbal and more with feeling.
- Jesus responds to Mary not with words but with feeling. ''When Jesus saw her weeping . . . He was troubled in spirit, moved by the deepest emotions.'' (Jn 11:33)   Jesus adapts Himself to Mary's personality.

I invite you to get in touch with your prayer life and, with the background of Mary's relationship with Jesus, become aware of your way of prayer:

- How do you pray?
- Do you feel the need to talk or do you quietly express your feelings and emotions to Jesus?
- Do you feel Jesus understands you?
- Are you satisfied with the way Jesus responds to you or do you want Him to deal with you as He does with others who are different from you?
- In your prayer life, do you compare yourself with others and feel insecure, uncertain of your holiness?
- Or do you relish and take delight in the fact that Jesus responds to your prayer according to your personality?

Mary showed her gratitude to Jesus, not in words but in deed. She "bought a pound of costly perfume made from genuine aromatic nard, with which she anointed Jesus' feet. Then she dried His feet with her hair, and the house was filled with the ointment's fragrance." (Jn 12:3)

Before you end your prayer, take a few moments and experience the deeply felt love Jesus has for you as you relive in imagination some meaningful events in your life.

Become consciously aware of the way you expressed your gratitude to Him. As you feel right now, renew your gratitude to Jesus and thank Him for all His love for you and for the life-giving relationship you have with Him.

When you are ready, gently end the exercise.

28.
NICODEMUS
(John 3:1-21, 19:39-42)

ST. JOHN PRESENTS Nicodemus as a "Pharisee . . . a member of the Jewish Sanhedrin [who] came to [Jesus] at night." (Jn 3:1-2) In your prayer, become aware of your similarities with Nicodemus:

- What kind of Christian/Catholic are you?
- Are you a Christian only by name or do you actually live your faith and beliefs?
- Is your living faith just a personal relationship with Jesus or do you actively take part in the Church's ministry and activity?
- What makes you an active member of the Church and, if you are not active, what hinders you from actively sharing your faith with others?

In his heart, Nicodemus accepted Jesus as a Rabbi, yet he was afraid to declare this acceptance publicly. He came to Jesus at night so that no one would know of his discipleship. As you look at your friendships and relationships:

- Are you open with others about your faith, religious beliefs and Church membership or do you keep these gifts just within yourself?
- What causes you to be silent, uncooperative and withdrawn when faith and religion are discussed?
- Is it fear, human respect, lack of knowledge?
- Or is it because your faith in and love of Jesus are shallow?
- What ways and means can you use to publicly show and freely share who is Jesus for you and what faith means to you?
- Where and how deeply rooted are your faith in and discipleship with Jesus?
- Take a couple of moments with Jesus as you get in touch with the roots of your faith and the depth of your discipleship.

Nicodemus believed that Jesus is "a teacher come from God" (Jn 3:2)   and, being a teacher of the law himself, he came to Jesus to deepen and purify his knowledge:

- Do you really believe that Jesus is God since ". . . no one can perform signs and wonders such as you perform unless God is with Him"? (Jn 3:2)
- What is YOUR experience of Jesus, the teacher?
- What teachings of Jesus do you find easy, acceptable, agreeable, and follow?
- What teachings do you find hard, disagreeable, senseless and difficult to follow?
- In the hard and difficult teachings of Jesus, do you just give up and live in ignorance?
- Or do you, like Nicodemus, ask questions, seek clarification and take risks?

Doubts about faith and questions about the Church are not a sign of disbelief. As Nicodemus strengthened his belief because of the answers of Jesus, so will you grow in intimacy with the Lord if only you humbly and prayerfully place your doubts and lack of understanding in the heart of Jesus:

- What aspects of the faith do not allow you to have full peace of soul? Talk about them to Jesus.
- What troubles you in the institutional Church — the renewed liturgy, parish committees, letters from the hierarchy. . . .?
- Take some time and share your frustrations and irritations with Jesus and listen to what He has to say to you about such pain.

As you look at yourself, is your faith based:

- On what others have taught you?
- On what your parents and teachers passed on to you?
- On your personal convictions because of experiences you had?
- On the unconditional and personal love of Jesus for you?

Nicodemus grew in his love for Jesus and ultimately showed publicly that he was His disciple when he "likewise came, bringing a mixture of myrrh and aloes which weighed about a hundred pounds" and anointed the body of Jesus and buried it in the tomb. (Jn 19:40-42)   As you look at your Christian witnessing today:

- What convinces you that your faith in Jesus is strong and growing?
- What stages do you see in the growth of your faith life as you live it today?
- Are you fully satisfied with:

    - Your interior faith and relationship with Jesus?

- The way you express and share your faith in your family, at work and in worship?
- Your activity in recognition of and gratitude for the gift of faith?

Before you end the prayer, spend a few moments with Jesus. As you are in touch with your faith and the way you live and share it with others, thank Jesus for all that He means to you. Ask Him to strengthen and encourage you to do what needs to be done to be another Nicodemus not only at night but also during the days of your life. When you are ready, gently end the exercise.

29.

THE WOULD-BE DISCIPLES
(Luke 9:57-62)

I INVITE YOU to imagine yourself walking with Jesus early in the morning on a road leading to Jerusalem. You heard His teaching, witnessed a miracle and now want to be with Him a little longer. Become aware of your feelings and thoughts as you walk next to Jesus, listening to what He is saying.

As you walk along, someone says to Jesus, "I will be your follower wherever you go." Immediately Jesus answers him, "The foxes have lairs, the birds of the sky have nests, but the Son of Man has nowhere to lay His head." (Lk 9:57-58)

- Do you know who this person is who wants to follow Jesus wherever He goes?
- What qualities and strengths made this person desire to follow Jesus?

- What, in your opinion, caused Jesus to give His immediate and somewhat discouraging answer?
- Was it some weakness in the person or perhaps to alert many who were with Him?
- What is YOUR reaction to this experience?
- Share it with Jesus, especially if you see something of yourself in what is happening.

After a short stretch of silent walking, Jesus stops at a person who was walking toward Him and tells him, "Come after me." The person hesitantly answers Him, "Let me bury my father first." To which Jesus replies, "Let the dead bury their dead; come away and proclaim the Kingdom of God." (Lk 9:59-60)

In imagination, relive this scene:

- Where is Jesus as He meets this person?
- How old is this person? What is his family like?
- Are you surprised that Jesus stops and calls this person and wants him to "come away and proclaim the Kingdom of God"?
- What feelings, emotions and thoughts arise within you as you experience all this?
- Do you see anything of yourself in this event, times when Jesus called you directly to "come away" and you found it hard to oblige promptly?
- If Jesus were to turn to you right now and call you to "come away" with Him, what would your response be?
- Turn to Jesus, let your heart communicate your feelings and be grateful.

As you continue your journey with Jesus, one of the group comes near Jesus, touches Him and tells Him, "Lord, I will be your follower, but first let me take leave of my people at home."

After a short while, Jesus answers this person, "Whoever puts his hand to the plough but keeps looking back is unfit for the reign of God." (Lk 9:61-62)

Look at the face of this person and try to feel what he is feeling as he listens to the answer of Jesus:

- What desires did this person have that urged him to become a follower?
- What made him stop Jesus and express his desire for discipleship?
- How strong were his attachments that caused him to place conditions on discipleship?
- What did this person do after hearing the strong response of Jesus?
- As you observe all that is happening, become aware of what is happening within you: feelings, thoughts, emotions, desires, the past and the present.
- Go near Jesus and let Him talk to you about what is happening within you right now.

Before you end the prayer, take a few moments and, as you go back to what happened right now, check yourself:

- Do you identify yourself with any of the three persons in the journey?
- To what extent do you identify yourself?
- What helped you to put aside any conditions to follow Jesus?
- Who and what influenced you to trust and hope, to let go of fears and let Jesus into your life?
- As Jesus continues to invite you and call you to "come away and proclaim the Kingdom of God," what answer do you give Him?
- Take a few moments of quiet reflection on what happened in this prayer exercise, share your feelings with Jesus and, when you are ready, gently end the exercise.

30.
THE SEVENTY-TWO DISCIPLES

(Luke 10:1-12)

I INVITE YOU to place yourself with Jesus, surrounded by many followers, as He chooses seventy-two of them and sends them on a mission.

"The Lord appointed a further seventy-two." (Lk 10:1)

Imagine yourself among the followers of Jesus and see Jesus coming to the group. Listen to His greeting and short message. See Him looking at you and listen to Him calling and choosing YOU from among the group:

- How big is the group of followers of Jesus?
- Where are you in the group? Are you visible, somewhat in front or hidden at the back?
- Let Jesus look at you and, as you return the look, listen to Him calling you by name.
- What feelings arise within you as you hear your name clearly and loudly called?
- Move forward toward Jesus and experience the feelings and thoughts of Jesus toward you.

"He sent them in pairs before Him to every town and place He intended to visit." (Lk 10:1)

As Jesus chooses the seventy-two, He forms pairs to send you on your mission. Observe Jesus calling people and forming pairs:

- Do you know any of these pairs of people?
- Whom does Jesus give you as a companion for your mission?
- Is she/he your spouse, a friend, an unknown person?

- Do you like this person and does this person like you?
- Are you grateful for your choice and for the companion given to you?
- Thank Jesus for your mission and for His choice of both of you.
- What memories and feelings from daily life does all this bring to you?

Jesus says to you, "The harvest is rich but the workers are few; therefore ask the harvest-master to send workers to his harvest." (Lk 10:2)

The first mission that Jesus gives you is to pray for workers:

- Are you aware of the vastness of the harvest to which you are sent?
- To what people and places are you sent to minister?
- Do you pray with faith for priestly and religious vocations?
- Or do you blame the institutionalism of the Church for the lack of vocations?
- What are you doing for vocations at home, in the parish and at work?

"I am sending you as lambs in the midst of wolves." (Lk 10:3) "You must be clever as snakes and innocent as doves." (Mt 10:16)

Looking at the way you live your mission in the Church and in society:

- How often do you face wolves as you fulfill your mission?
- Who and what are these wolves:
  - Are they people without faith, hard-hearted people, broken people?
  - Or are they situations and events in life that challenge your spirituality?

- With what people do you have to be clever and innocent so as to let Jesus be proclaimed and accepted?
- Experience an event when you felt sent by God as a lamb among wolves and thank Jesus for the growth you have experienced.

"Do not carry a walking staff or traveling bag; wear no sandals and greet no one along the way." (Lk 10:4)

To help you realize that it is His mission you are doing on earth, Jesus asks full trust from you. In practice:

- Do you count on your human gifts, natural qualities or material riches?
- Or do you use all this and put your whole trust in the Lord?
- How attached are you to success as you fulfill your mission?
- Or are you satisfied that you are trying your best to do God's will in life?

"On entering any house, first say, 'Peace to this house.' . . . Into whatever city you go, after they welcome you, eat what they set before you, and cure the sick there. Say to them, 'The reign of God is at hand.' " (Lk 10:5, 8-9)

Looking at your ministry in your family, in the Church and in society:

- Do you always bring peace to all you meet?
- What feedback do you get from people as they talk about you as a person of peace?

A part of your mission in life is to make others aware of God's life in them and to bring them healing. Take a moment and become aware of:

- Ways in which you make people aware that God lives in them and loves them.

- What do you say or do to them that opens their heart to healing and new life?
- Have you ever experienced a healing power coming out of you as you shared the compassion and forgiveness of Jesus?
- Was this just your human quality or the power of Jesus working in you?

Before you end the prayer, take a few moments of intimacy with Jesus:

- Become aware of the mission that He gave you.
- Bring to your heart the people who are entrusted to your care.
- As different feelings and movements arise within you, turn to Jesus and renew your commitment to Him.
- Ask Him to help you persevere in your mission.
- When you are ready, gently end the exercise.

31.
THE FARSIGHTED STEWARD
(Luke 12:32-48)

IMAGINE Jesus in front of you and listen to His teaching. As a human being, you are entrusted with the stewardship of your life. This stewardship implies certain requirements.

"Let your belts be fastened around your waists and your lamps be burning ready." (Lk 12:35) Get in touch with the talents, qualities and skills that make you the person you are:

- Are you aware of the true, rich self that you are?
- How much of this richness do you accept?

- Have you deepened, enriched and strengthened your personality through education, training and use?
- What do you do to "let your lamps burn" and "keep your belt fastened" daily?
- Are you responsibly active or lazily passive?

"Be like people awaiting their master's return . . . so that . . . you will open for him without delay." (Lk 12:36)   Awaiting and promptness show one's readiness and alertness to respond. Look at your daily behavior and relationships with others:

- Are you so alert to others' needs that you respond promptly and generously?
- Are your responsibilities in life sufficiently fulfilled so that you can peacefully await the Master's coming at any time?
- Or are you such a procrastinator that you fear His coming?
- What do you need to do, correct or improve to patiently await and promptly open when demands are made on you?

"Do not live in fear, little flock. . . . Get purses for yourselves that do not wear out." (Lk 12:32-33)

- Is your life directed by anxiety, fear and duty or by peace, freedom and love?
- What are your guiding principles in all that you do, say and choose?
- Do your ambitions and ideals give you a passing satisfaction or do they give you a deep sense of well-being and spiritual growth?

Jesus looks at you lovingly and clearly makes known to you His expectations.
"When much has been given to you, much will be required of you. More will be asked of one to whom more has been entrusted."

(Lk 12:48)   Become aware of the blessings and graces with which you are enriched:

- How richly have you been blessed? Has ''very much'' been given to you?
- Name your physical, emotional, spiritual and psychological blessings.
- Name your human gifts and qualities and acquired skills.
- How do you compare the quality and quantity of your use and sharing of your riches with the worth of the gifts themselves?
- Are you satisfied or uncomfortable with your lack of effort, procrastination or taking things for granted?
- Do you therefore try to ''be on guard'' (Lk 12:40)   trying not only to accept your gifts but also to use them responsibly, generously and willingly?

The farsighted stewards who are responsible and generous in the fulfillment of their duties are highly rewarded by the Master.

''He will put on an apron, seat them at table, and proceed to wait on them.'' (Lk 12:37)   ''His Master will put him in charge of all His property.'' (12:44)

Once more, become aware of your blessings, the way you use your gifts and the effect of all this in your life. As you look at your life:

- Do you have any factual experiences that show you that Jesus has rewarded you for all that you have done?
- From your experiences, how do you explain Jesus ''seating you at table'' and ''waiting on you''?
- Take a few moments and relive a few events when you felt Jesus loving and serving you because you accepted and used His love.
- How does this generous love affect your efforts to grow in intimacy with Jesus and in loving your neighbor?

- What does it mean to you that Jesus "will put you in charge of all His property"?
- Does it mean peace, spiritual freedom, a balanced and integrated personality?

Before you end the exercise, take a few moments of loving dialogue with Jesus and:

- Thank Him for all that He shares with you and for His lavish goodness to you.
- Ask Him to produce in you a grateful heart that sings:

"The Lord has done great things for me, I am glad indeed." (Ps 126:3)

"What return shall I make to the Lord for all the good He has done for me?" (Ps 116:12)

32.
ZECHARIAH

(Luke 1)

ZECHARIAH WAS A PRIEST, married to Elizabeth. Both lived good lives, were very old and had no children because Elizabeth was infertile.

While performing his priestly duties in the temple, Zechariah had a vision of an angel of God who told him: "Do not be frightened, Zechariah, your prayer has been heard. Your wife Elizabeth shall bear a son whom you shall name John." (Lk 1:13)

I invite you to live this event in imagination. Get in touch with:

- Zechariah's holiness and priestly privilege to burn incense at the altar.
- Zechariah's old age and his having no children.
- The life-long prayers of the couple to have a child.

Experience also the feelings of Zechariah as the angel gives him the unexpected news. Feelings of unbelief, of the impossible, almost of ridicule.

Yet, as the angel tells Zechariah that he and many others will rejoice at his child's birth because ". . . he will be great in the eyes of the Lord . . . and he will be filled with the Holy Spirit from his mother's womb" (Lk 1:15), experience the doubts and the many questions that pass through Zechariah's heart and mind.

Center your attention on your life. You may be married or single, priest or religious:

- Was there ever in your heart a strong desire to achieve or do something and you never had that desire fulfilled?
- What did you do and how, hopefully, did you pray to have this desire fulfilled?
- Do you still trust that some day this desire will be fulfilled or have you lost hope?
- Look intently at your life and see if Zechariah's vision brings to the surface something in your life.
- If something surfaces, become aware of how you have accepted THIS event and how you dealt with it.

Although the angel made it clear that this child will be a gift from the Lord, born for a special mission, Zechariah did not believe it would happpen. He was too engrossed in his human limitations.

"How am I to know this? I am an old man; my wife too is advanced in age." (Lk 1:18)

As a result of his unbelief, Zechariah was punished. "You will be mute — unable to speak — until the day these things take place." (Lk 1:20)

Get in touch with events in your life when you lacked faith, when you thought only of your human resources and put aside any possible initiative from God. In such events:

- Did you listen carefully to what the Lord was telling you?
- Or were you lost in the humanness and materiality of the event?
- Did you allow exterior factors of the events to darken the inner brightness of your faith?
- As you look back, what clues did you have that what was happening to you was directed by Divine Providence?
- Did you receive any correction or punishment for your unbelief?
- Or was the Lord merciful to you, leading you patiently to open up to Him?

In spite of Zechariah's unbelief, Elizabeth conceived in her old age and gave birth to a son. She intervened saying: "No, he is to be called John." (Lk 1:60) As Zechariah wrote the words, "His name is John" (1:63), he was able to speak again. He was filled with the Holy Spirit and prophesied about the mission of his newborn son. (1:67-79)

As you ponder the gift of speech regained by Zechariah and his proclamation of God's praise, become aware of times when, even though you did not believe that what you desired would come true, it did happen in due time:

- Did your desire come true directly . . . as you wanted it?
- Or did you get your answer through a different grace, gift or event?
- What signs do you have that your prayers were answered?
- Are your reactions similar to Zechariah's or are you still angry that things did not happen exactly when and how you wanted?

- Experience the power of the Lord in what is happening to you, let your tongue loosen up and let it express loudly what your heart is feeling.
- Allow the Spirit of Jesus to inundate and inebriate you and let Him sanctify you, as you offer Him all that you are and have in silent adoration.
- When you are ready, gently end the exercise.

33.
PILATE

(John 18:28-19:16)

PONTIUS PILATE is a person who draws our prayerful attention because, many a time, we can easily identify with him. He was a Roman Procurator before whom Jesus was brought for judgment. Pilate comes across to us as a person whose compromise cost him a painful struggle.

Pilate was sensitive to both Jesus and the Jewish crowds, and he did not like to get involved. His problem was that he HAD to decide. In silence, let the word ''compromise'' become alive in you:

- What thoughts or feelings does ''compromise'' evoke in you?
- Does ''compromise'' unfold to you any memories or experiences in your life?
- What facts, people, decisions did you compromise with in life?
- Was compromising a painful struggle or an easy decision to make?
- Look at yourself compromising . . . then look at Pilate and allow your imagination to open you to prayer.

Compromise happens because there is a strong attraction to two realities. Pilate was faced with the innocent Jesus and with his self-love.

Pilate was sensitive to Jesus and, in a truthful dialogue, recognized the innocence of Jesus.

'' 'Are you the King of the Jews? . . . What have you done? . . . So, then, you are a king?' . . . Jesus replied . . . 'Anyone committed to the truth hears my voice.' '' (Jn 18:33-37)

Reflecting on similar situations in your life:

- How open were you to listen to all people involved and to both sides of the problem?
- Was there any bias or previous influence that hindered you from accepting the whole truth?
- How did this truthfulness influence your judgment and actions?

Pilate was convinced that Jesus was innocent. Again and again, he said this: "Speaking for myself, I find no cause against this man." (Jn 18:38) "I am going to bring him out to you to make you realize that I find no case against Him." (19:4) "Take Him and crucify Him yourselves; I find no case against Him." (19:6) "After this, Pilate was eager to release Him." (19:12)

- How often in life, because of your honesty, were you convinced of truth, goodness and right?
- What brought you to this conviction and helped you to act accordingly?
- Did you follow this truth, right and goodness or did you compromise because of other realities?
- Why did these other realities hinder you from following the truth and right?

Pilate had to compromise because he did not like to get involved. He was afraid. "Why do you not take Him and pass judgment on Him according to your law?" (Jn 18:31)

As you look at different turning points in your life:

- Do you feel there were times when you shunned getting involved?
- What made you shun involvement: fear, lack of interest, loss of prestige?
- Has this weakness led you to failure and destruction?
- Or have you challenged it and overcome yourself?

Compromise led Pilate into a painful struggle. He was afraid of the crowds yet he knew that Jesus was innocent. Hanging between these strong realities, he:

- Tried to release Jesus by comparing Him to Barabbas. (Jn 18:39)
- Scourged Jesus, without any case against Him. (19:1)
- Appealed to the crowd's compassion. (19:4-5)
- Repeatedly questioned Jesus as if to find a reason to release Him. (18:33-38)

As you look at your life, choose an event when you compromised and when this compromise caused you agony. Take some time and:

- Go back to the different stages and various techniques you used to come out of the problem.
- Experience your inadequacy and helplessness.
- Feel the Lord's wisdom and guidance.
- Feel the struggle to decide.
- Spend some time with Jesus as you relive this struggle again.

Because Pilate feared the crowds and loved himself and Caesar more than Jesus, he put aside all right reasoning and gave in to his selfish attachment. ''In the end, Pilate handed Jesus over to be crucified.'' (Jn 19:16)

- How often does group pressure influence your decisions in the wrong way?
- What are the fears and loves that hinder you from doing what is right?
- What pain and evil have you caused to others by your compromises in life?
- Do you regret your compromises, fears and possessive attachments?
- What do you intend to do in the future?

Before you end the exercise, take a few moments and unburden your heart to Jesus, your Savior and Redeemer. Ask Him to wash you clean and to strengthen you in fighting all compromises in life.

34.
THE BENT-OVER WOMAN
(Luke 13:10-17)

IN THE SILENCE of your heart, I invite you to become the bent-over person in the gospel event. Take some time and imagine yourself bent-over. Get a feel of your body in this position and experience its uncomfortable effects on you.

As you get in touch with your bent-over position, try to remember:

- Since when did you know yourself as a bent-over person?
- What made you bent-over? An illness? An accident? A deficiency?
- Do you experience any difference in your attitudes, behavior or thought since you became bent-over?

- How do people treat you or relate to you as a bent-over person?
- Can you imagine being bent-over for the rest of your life?
- What feelings, memories or emotions arise within you as you accept your bent-over position, and what are your responses to these feelings?

Now try to become consciously aware of the real cause that made you a bent-over person:

- What bends you over, denying you the privilege of looking at people and things straight in the face?
- Is the weight that bends you over physical? moral? social? sociological?
- Feel the burden that enslaves you and name the burden or burdens.

Having named the weight that bends you over, feel the EFFECT that your body and spirit suffer because of it. Name these painful effects that are inflicted on you:

- Become aware of your physical inconveniences.
- How is your psyche affected now that you can never look straight ahead but only at the ground?
- What effect is this having on your general attitude to life and to your relationships?
- Is your bent-over deficiency affecting your prayer life?
- What feelings, emotions or desires unfold themselves to you as you experience these painful effects?

There are times when being bent-over does not feel too bad. In fact, you may tend to get used to its advantages even though you have to pay the price for them.

Take some time and ask yourself if this is true in your case, at least occasionally.

1. There might be times when you like to be bent-over because you do not want people to look at you straight in the face. PRIDE can make this happen.

   - Do you feel so burdened, broken and humiliated with repeated weaknesses and failures that you do not have the courage to let people look you in the face?
   - Are you so ashamed of yourself that pride makes it easier for you to remain bent-over rather than straight, honest and sincere?
   - Do you feel so inferior and insecure that it becomes a natural inclination to be bent-over and away from strengths that can straighten you up?

2. There might be times when you like to be bent-over because you want people to keep bending over towards you and pitying you. COMFORT can make this happen.

   - Do you feel pleased and comfortable as a bent-over person because this makes others give you attention, compassion and help?
   - What makes this craving for attention worth paying the painful price?
   - Do you prefer to remain in this situation, calling people to bend over to you instead of you straightening up?

3. There might be times when you like to be bent-over because it is too painful to straighten up. WEAKNESS and BROKENNESS can make this happen.

   - Have you allowed your weaknesses to overcome you and lord it over you?
   - Are your weaknesses so strong that you do not have the strength to fight them?
   - In this case, *you need someone very strong* to bend over to your level to pull you up and straighten you up.

Surely this is very hard and painful because by straightening up you will lose the limited security and safe seclusion that you enjoy. Yet this strong Someone is present right now in front of you. JESUS who created you straight is ready to straighten you up again, if you are willing:

- Do you want to straighten up? To look others in the face?
- Do you want others to look you in the face, or are you comfortable and want to remain bent-over?

Being and walking straight is ultimately a gift of God. As you are in front of Jesus, ask Him to bend over to you, raise your head towards Him and let Him lift you up, raise you and straighten you up:

- As you ask for healing with deep faith, feel the pain of being straightened up and let go of the attachments that weigh you down and bend you over.
- Feel the energy coming within you as you allow the blood to circulate in your veins and your joints to move smoothly as you straighten up.
- Feel yourself straight once again and enjoy the power within you as you walk straight and are able to see straight and to look at people straight in the face.

Take a few moments, as you gently end the exercise:

- To thank Jesus for His healing power as He stoops down to you. (Ps 40:2)
- Ask Him to continue touching and straightening you as you meet with small painful or attractive experiences that tend to bend you over again. (Ps 40:14)
- You may end the prayer by praying Psalm 40.

35.

THE GRATEFUL LEPER
(Luke 17:11-19)

IMAGINE YOURSELF one of the ten lepers who met Jesus at the border between Samaria and Galilee on His way to Jerusalem.

Get a feel for yourself: sick, secluded from family and neighbors, perhaps living in a restricted place:

- Where do you stand today emotionally, physically, psychologically?
- Are you alone or do you live with other sick people?
- Is your sickness spiritual, physical, emotional?
- Is alcohol or drug abuse, overeating or pleasure-seeking a part of your sickness?
- Does your sickness affect other areas of your life?
- How does it affect your marriage or family/community life?
- Become aware of yourself as a sick person and be in touch with your pain, loneliness, discouragement and helplessness.

Imagine Jesus coming toward you as you feel sick and abandoned. Look at Him and get in touch with His feelings and attitude:

- How do you see Jesus as He approaches?
- What does the distance between you and Jesus signify in your life?
- Where was this distance born and what made it grow?
- Look at Jesus as He approaches the place where you are and become aware of what attracts you to ask Him for healing.

"Keeping their distance, they raised their voices and said, 'Jesus, Master, have pity on us.' " (Lk 17:12-13)   By staying at a distance these persons accepted their dreaded disease:

- Do you accept your sicknesses, pains and hurts?
- Name the sicknesses that burden you.
- Are you comfortable with them or do you, in humility, seek to be healed?
- Do you really want to be healed and cleansed?
- With great trust, ask Jesus: "Lord, take pity on me."

"When He saw them, He responded, 'Go and show yourselves to the priests.' " (Lk 17:14)   Allow Jesus to look at you, place your own request to Him and listen to Him answering you:

- How does Jesus look at you?
- What effect does the look of Jesus have on your heart?
- What exactly does Jesus say to you?
- As Jesus touches your heart and senses, feel His cleansing power.

"One of them, realizing that he had been cured . . . threw himself on his face at the feet of Jesus and spoke His praises." (Lk 17:15-16)   As you look at the healing and cleansing moments in your life, become aware of your reactions:

- Are they reactions of forgetfulness, taking things for granted or are they reactions of gratitude?
- After the first emotions, do you ever reflect on what really happened to you?
- Has your reflection ever changed your carelessness into gratitude?

I now invite you to go back to the experience you just had and, from it, go back to other healings the Lord has offered you:

- Relive a few of these healing experiences.
- Experience the power and love of Jesus within you.
- Realize how, without Jesus, you would have never been healed and forgiven.
- Allow feelings of gratitude to arise within you and, either in word or in gesture, express your gratitude to Jesus in loving adoration.

Jesus is happy that you return to Him to offer thanks. Ingratitude is painful: "Were not all ten made whole? Where are the other nine?" (Lk 17:17)

Gratitude is a gift of God, a blessing of an active faith. Before you end your prayer spend some time in prayerful reflection and, in imagination, go back to the past six months:

- Become aware of people who were really good to you, especially in moments of need.
- Become aware of some special good, blessing or event that happened to you.
- Remember how you expressed gratitude to God and to others for what happened to you.
- If you were negligent or forgetful in giving thanks, take a few moments now and:

  - Thank Jesus for what He gave you and allowed you to experience in life.
  - Think what you can do to show gratitude to people who are good to you.
  - When you are ready, gently end the exercise as Jesus touches you and tells you: "Stand up and go your way; your faith has been your salvation." (Lk 17:19)

36.

THE REPENTANT CRIMINAL
(Luke 23:39-43)

IMAGINE JESUS in His agony on the cross. Get a feel of the place. See Jesus and the two criminals on their crosses. Look at the crowd and listen to their angry shouting.

Allow Jesus to become the center of your attention. Realize how in the midst of such suffering and abandonment, He suffers silently because He loves you. As you look at Jesus on the cross:

- What thoughts and feelings arise in you?
- How does the silent suffering of Jesus, compared with the loud anger of the crowd, affect you?
- Are your thoughts and emotions turned toward Jesus, the crowd or yourself?

Listen to the criminal blaspheming: "Aren't you the Messiah? Then save yourself and us." (Lk 23:39)   Recognize the sincere repentance of the other criminal as he says: "Have you no fear of God, seeing you are under the same sentence? We deserve it, after all. We are only paying the price for what we've done." (23:40-41)

In your prayer try to identify with the repentant criminal who by admitting his wrongdoing knew that he was suffering for the evil he did. Look at your thoughts, feelings and behavior:

- Where do you see imperfection, failure and sin in your words, deeds and thoughts?
- What are your sins? Where do you sin most?
- What causes you to fall again and again?

- Do you sin because you are strong or because you are weak?
- Do you admit your sinfulness or do you refuse to accept that you are a sinner?
- Keeping in mind your sinfulness, look at Jesus dying on the cross and become aware of your feelings.

The criminal was aware that Jesus was innocent. ". . . but this man has done nothing wrong." (Lk 23:41)   Having experienced the loving compassion of Jesus, the criminal repented of his sins and asked for forgiveness: "Jesus, remember me when you enter upon your reign." (23:42)

You are aware of your sinfulness and you also believe that you are so precious in the sight of God that you are worth the passion and death Jesus endured for you. Take a few moments and:

- With sincere sorrow, offer all your failures and sins to Jesus.
- With great trust, join the criminal in asking Jesus for purification.
- As you place your past in the heart of Jesus, let Him wash it clean with His blood.
- In humble repentance, experience the peace of soul and the cleanliness of heart that Jesus offers you.

The repentant criminal was instantly rewarded by Jesus: "I assure you: this day you will be with Me in paradise." (Lk 23:43)

Before you end the prayer, I invite you to spend a few moments reflecting on the sacrament of reconciliation:

- Do you really understand what a great gift Jesus has offered you in this sacrament?
- In this sacrament have you ever experienced true healing of soul?
- How do you compare the fruit of this spiritual healing with that of psychological counseling?
- Do you see this sacrament as a burden, a humiliation, a confirmation of your pride?

- Or do you see in it a repeated renewal of Christ's love for you and a constant proof that Christianity is the religion where a new beginning is always possible?

As you end your prayer, relive in imagination an experience you had where you sincerely felt that Jesus forgave you:

- Feel again your sincere sorrow for sin, the healing touch of Jesus and the peace of soul you then felt.
- Thank Jesus for giving you the sacrament of reconciliation.
- Ask Him to deepen your faith in the sacrament so that, every time you need to use it, you will truly hear Jesus telling you: "I assure you that one day you, too, will be with Me in paradise."

37.
THE PENITENT WOMAN
(Luke 7:36-50)

AFTER READING the above Scripture passage, I invite you to become the penitent woman and relive the scene in imagination:

- Where is Simon's house built? How richly furnished is it?
- What kind of person is Simon the Pharisee?
- What made Simon invite Jesus for this dinner?

Having learned that Jesus is at Simon's house, let your desire to meet Jesus grow within you. Start moving toward the house. Enter the dining room where Jesus reclines at the table:

- How big is this room? Where is the table placed? How is it set for dinner?

- Look at the people reclining at the table. How many are there?
- Whom do you know and recognize?

As you see certain people, your sense of shame and confusion wells up within you as you remember previous experiences:

- Who, among the group, causes this shame to arise within you?
- What are your first reactions to this sense of shame?
- Do you want to run away?
- Who and what urged you to come to this room?
- Yes, Jesus is at the head of the table and you have to cross the whole room to go near Him.
- Let the strong urge within you move your feet toward Jesus as your eyes and heart are fixed on Him.

You have come to this room with the sole purpose of meeting Jesus. You are afraid, ashamed of your past and discouraged at the sight of some guests. Yet the loving gaze of Jesus toward you drew you to His feet.

Compose yourself and, as you experience shame for the past and courage for the present moment, unfold your heart and your whole being to Jesus. In the silence of your heart and the loudness of your actions, turn to Jesus, kneel at His feet, open the perfume bottle and let the deep sorrow for your sins show itself in:

- The grateful perfuming of His feet.
- The heartfelt tears that rush from your eyes.
- The gentle caresses your hands offer to His feet.
- The kisses of purified repentance.
- The wiping of the perfume with your hair.
- Take your time and let your inner repentance for your sins and the deepfelt forgiveness of Jesus show themselves in your silent yet very loud and open confession. Talk to Jesus in the silence of your heart.

You have done what you wanted to. Now, renewed and strengthened by the healing touch of Jesus your Savior-Friend, lift up your eyes and look at the guests reclining at the table. Look at Simon the host:

- How does he look at you?
- Can you detect what he is thinking and feeling about you?
- Look straight at his eyes and let your heart speak to his heart.

Right now, Jesus sits straight, places His left arm around your shoulders and starts talking to Simon and the other guests:

- Feel the warmth and the firm hold of Jesus' hands around your shoulders.
- Listen to what Jesus is saying to Simon.
- Become aware of the pin-drop silence as all eyes are turned to Jesus.
- What feelings and emotions arise in you as you hear Jesus telling Simon:
  - "She has washed My feet with her tears and wiped them with her hair." (Lk 7:44)
  - "She has not ceased kissing My feet since I entered." (7:45)
  - "She has anointed My feet with perfume." (7:46)
  - "Because of her great love, her many sins are forgiven." (7:47)
- Take your time, listen again and again to Jesus, feel His touch going deeper and deeper into your whole being, healing you, purifying you, giving you new life. Let your heart and soul and body prostrate themselves at the feet of Jesus in grateful adoration for His public forgiveness as He tells you, "Your sins are forgiven." (Lk 7:48) "Your faith has been your salvation. Now go in peace." (7:50)

Remain with Jesus in grateful adoration for the gift of your repentance and newness of life. As you offer your new self to Jesus, listen to what He has to tell you. End your prayer by a loving embrace as Jesus looks lovingly at you.

38.

SIMON, THE PHARISEE
(Luke 7:36-50)

AFTER READING the above Scripture passage, I invite you to become Simon, the host, and relive the scene in imagination. As Simon:

- Become aware of your house, especially the banquet room where dinner is going to take place.
- How did you want the room to be decorated and how did you order the table to be set?
- Whom, besides Jesus, did you invite for dinner, and where have you seated them?
- As you look at the room and the table set for dinner, what feelings and thoughts arise within you?

The appointed time comes and the guests start coming. As different guests enter the house, become aware of:

- What person he/she is . . . your attitude toward her/him . . . and their response to your invitation.
- Jesus, your special guest.
- What feelings and emotions do you experience as you meet Him face to face?

- What do you say to or do for Him as He enters your house?
- What response do you get from Him?
- As you welcome and greet Jesus, are you also aware of the other guests?
- Do you want to impress them that Jesus is your special guest?
- What is happening within you as you know your intentions?

As introductions are made and the guests take their place at the table, a woman, publicly known as a sinner, enters the room. After a short pause near the door, she comes up to Jesus. She kneels at His feet and pays her respect in her unique way:

- What is your reaction to the woman's presence?
- Do you wish to throw her out and disgrace her publicly?
- Or do you control yourself and wait for the others' reactions?
- As you look at the other guests, what expressions do you see on their faces?
- Are their expressions similar or different from yours?
- What makes you wait and tolerate the woman's behavior toward Jesus?

Though you succeed in controlling your actions, your thoughts are very active and so much is passing through your mind:

- What are you thinking right now about the woman?
- How do the expressions on the guests' faces affect you?
- Deep down in your heart, what are you saying to the woman? to Jesus?
- What judgments do your heart and mind make about the woman? About Jesus?

While this goes on, Jesus sits straight, looks into your eyes and, with a strong voice tells you, "Simon, I have something to propose to you." (Lk 7:40)

- What is happening to you as Jesus addresses you directly?
- How do you feel when Jesus tells you, "You are right." (Lk 7:43)?

Jesus continues to talk to you and tells you:

- "I came to your house and you provided Me with no water for My feet." (Lk 7:44)
- "You gave Me no kiss." (7:45)
- "You did not anoint My head with oil." (7:46)
- "Little is forgiven the one whose love is small." (7:47)

As these words sink into your heart and mind:

- What feelings do you experience: Are you ashamed? afraid? Do you feel ridiculed?
- What have you to say to Jesus? How do you respond?
- Do you regret that you have invited Jesus?
- What do you learn from all this?

Now become yourself again and, being enriched with the experience of Simon, I invite you to look at your relationship with Jesus and your neighbor:

- How honest, deep and sincere is your relationship with Jesus?
- Do you do all that you can to grow in your love for and imitation of Jesus?
- Or are you satisfied with the exterior fulfillment of rules and precepts?
- Is your love for Jesus an exterior show full of pride?
- Or a humble and interior search for true love?
- Get in touch with your living faith and open your heart to Jesus, the Lord.

Look at your relationship with your neighbor:

- Can you say that you are a true imitator of Jesus' love and compassion?
- What messages do you give to others and how do others see you?
- Is your relationship with others:

    - One of receiving and never giving?
    - One of self-sufficiency and pride?
    - One of acceptance of vulnerability and your need of others?
    - One that is a continual process of growth?

Before you end the prayer, become aware of what happened to you in this exercise, turn to Jesus and:

- Offer Him all your pride, wrong judgments, prejudices and pain that you caused to others.
- Ask Him to change your heart, to forgive you, heal and renew you.
- Ask Him for the grace of greater trust in His wise and loving guidance of your life.

39.

THE WIDOW OF NAIM
(Luke 7:11-17)

I INVITE YOU to become the widow of Naim and relive the consoling event she experienced. Become aware of:

- The woman, a widow, rather poor, heartbroken at the death of her son.

- The son, grown up, the only help of his mother, dead when most needed.
- The grieving of the mother, the compassionate support of the people.
- Jesus, moved with pity at the woman, raising her son to life.
- Hearing and praising God, the effect in those who witnessed the event.

As you relive this bittersweet experience, I invite you to look into your life and become aware of a sorrowful mystery in your life.

Being a Single Parent. Are you a single parent because of the death of your spouse or because of divorce?

1. If death is the reason, go through the stages that led you to this painful separation:
   - What sickness, pain and suffering did your partner have?
   - How painful was it for your partner and for you?
   - Experience the pain of separation and feel in you the spiritual, emotional, and social effects.

2. If divorce is the reason, go through the stages that led you to this painful decision:
   - Become aware of the first serious events that made you think of this painful situation.
   - What was the greatest pain that made you lose your peace of soul and happiness?
   - What attitudes, behavior and speech in the partner or in you convinced you to take this step?
   - What confusion, doubts, pain and anxiety did you experience as you sought this painful separation?
   - Who and what helped you to go through the ordeal, knowing it is for your good?
   - What signs and proofs did you see, and how did they convince you that your marriage was dead?

Loss of a child. If so:

- Did the loss happen because of carelessness, in an accident, or because of lack of appreciation or communication?
- Children are dear to you as a parent, yet are you aware that:
  - They do not belong to you but are only given to you as an enriching gift?
  - You cannot make of them an exact replica of yourself?
  - The more possessive and demanding you are, the greater the chance of losing them?
  - Being responsible for them does not mean controlling them?
  - Discipline has to be blended with love, respect and freedom in building them up?

Loss of a very good friend. If so:

- What brought you to this loss? Loneliness, insecurity and perhaps guilt?
- Look at your friendship and become aware of the reasons that brought about this loss: was it:
  - Your insecurity, over-dependence, infatuation, jealousy?
  - Too many differences in your backgrounds, education and characteristics?
  - Because you were always giving and never receiving, or vice-versa?
- Can you pinpoint the stages that led you to this precious loss?

Loss of your job. If so:

- Were you the only breadwinner in the family?
- How did this affect your self-esteem, your relationship with your spouse and children?

- How were your talents and skills affected because you were unable to use them?
- How did this affect your peace of soul and that of your family?
- Take a moment and be in touch with the sense of loss, separation and death and how all this affected your whole being.

". . . a dead man was being carried out . . . a considerable crowd of townsfolk were with her." (Lk 7:12)

As you experience your pain, loss or separation and as you carry it all in your heart, mind and body, do you feel:

- You are doing this by yourself, or are there others with you?
- Who are these others with you at this part of your painful journey?
- What do they do or say that comforts, encourages you or lightens your burden?
- Become aware of people who are true and loyal friends for you in time of need.
- Thank Jesus for so many people who prove a balm to your open wounds.

"The Lord was moved with pity upon seeing her and said to her, 'Do not cry' . . . He said, 'Young man, I bid you get up' . . . then Jesus gave him back to his mother." (Lk 7:13-15)

I invite you to become aware of yourself today, having gone through the trauma of your loss, separation or death:

- Do you see any traces of the presence of Jesus in whatever happened to you?
- How was Jesus present while you were sad, in pain, angry, anxious, guilty?
- At what moment in your trauma was Jesus "moved with pity" for you?

- Who or what made you feel deep within you the healing and renewing or reviving touch of Jesus?
- In what way or in whom did Jesus give you back or make up for what you have lost?

Before you end the exercise, take a few moments of loving dialogue with Jesus and, as you experience His presence in your life:

- Thank Him for all that He did for and with you in times of trial.
- Ask Him to continue sharing His merciful love with you.
- Praise Him for stopping at your home as He visits His people. (cf. Lk 7:16)

40.

THE PHARISEE AND THE TAX COLLECTOR

(Luke 18:9-14)

I INVITE YOU to imagine yourself present among a group of people listening to Jesus. The parable that Jesus uses today is "addressed to those who believed in their own self-righteousness." (Lk 18:9) Become aware of the place you are in, the people in the group and Jesus sitting in the middle:

- What attitude do you have as you look at different people in the group?
- What judgment do you pass on each person as they attract your attention?
- What feelings do you have toward each person: contempt, pity, compassion . . .?

Jesus starts talking: "Two men went up to the temple to pray; one was a Pharisee, the other a tax collector. The Pharisee with head unbowed prayed in this fashion: 'I give you thanks, O God, that I am not like the rest of men — grasping, crooked, adulterous — or even like this tax collector.' " (Lk 18:10-11)

Imagine yourself in your prayer group or community and all of you are praying:

- What posture do you use in prayer or does the posture mean nothing to you?
- What awareness do you have of each member in the community?
- How does this awareness affect your prayer?
- Does your prayer include others in the community? If yes,
- Whom do you include in your prayer: friends, relatives, enemies, broken people?
- Listen to yourself praying and become aware of:

   - What you are saying to God.
   - How you are praying (body-posture, heart and mind attitudes, faith).
   - The way you are praying for or about others.

- What feelings arise within you as you pray?
- Does Jesus answer your prayer? What does He tell you?
- Are you pleased and satisfied with your attitudes in prayer?

Direct your awareness to a couple of people who are praying with you and let something within them steal your attention:

- What do you see in these people that steals your attention?
- Is it the reverence they show, their body-language or is it some interior pull?
- Can you recognize their attitude toward God as they pray?
- Try to experience their feelings toward others as they pray for them.

- What do you learn as you go through this experience?
- What have you to say or do to any of them? Say it or do it now.

Jesus continues His parable. ''The other man, however, kept his distance, not even daring to raise his eyes to heaven. All he did was beat his breast and say: 'O God, be merciful to me, a sinner.' '' (Lk 18:13)

This person was fully aware of who he was, accepted his wrongdoing and humbly offered it to the Lord. The result was that he ''went home from the temple justified . . . for . . . he who humbles himself shall be exalted.'' (Lk 18:14)

As you look at your prayer life:

- Can you identify with this sinner's prayer?
- Are you aware of your failures and sins?
- Do you own and accept them as much as you own your strengths?
- Are you humble enough to give them to the Lord for purification?
- Or do you deny your weaknesses and hold to them in ignorance?
- Does your body language synchronize with your speech and your intentions?
- Or is your prayer a clear lie?

Take a few moments and look deep down into yourself and:

- Let your failures, addictions and sins unfold themselves to you.
- Own each one of them and feel how burdensome it is.
- See how each weakness is bringing about your spiritual death.
- As you recognize this dark and destructive aspect of your life, lift it up to Jesus in prayer.
- Then offer Him everything humbly and sorrowfully.
- Ask Him to forgive, purify and cleanse you.
- As you experience forgiveness and healing, spend a few moments of humble prayer at the foot of the crucified Lord.
- When you are ready, gently end the exercise.

41.
ZACCHAEUS

(Luke 19:1-10)

I INVITE YOU to be present at Zacchaeus' call and let his call unfold to you your own processes of calls and responses.

"There was a man there named Zacchaeus, the chief tax collector and a wealthy man." (Lk 19:2) This statement tells you who Zacchaeus was:

- The chief tax collector: a friend of the Romans with a suspicious personality because of his job.
- A wealthy man: probably despised by many because of the way he became rich.

Become aware of your personality traits and social standard:

- Are you a middle class person, enjoying most of life's comforts?
- How do people see you and what impressions do they have of you?
- Who are your friends and the people with whom you associate?
- What do people in general say about you?
- Does what people think and say about you correspond with who you really are?
- Are you pleased with the image that people have of you?

"He was trying to see what Jesus was like, but being small of stature, was unable to do so because of the crowd." (Lk 19:3)

However imperfect he was, Zacchaeus had a desire to meet Jesus and he did something about it. As you look at yourself:

- Can you name and own your weaknesses and imperfections?
- How do you accept these weaknesses?
- Do you allow them to destroy you or do you make them redemptive?
- Do you take the initiative to grow and improve?

Basically, Zacchaeus was a good man. He was determined to meet Jesus:

- What goodness do you possess?
- Are you convinced that you, too, are a good person?
- In living with your weaknesses and accepting pains, do you ever desire to meet Jesus?
- Is this desire a passing one or does it keep arising in your heart?

"He first ran on in front, then climbed a sycamore tree which was along Jesus' route, in order to see Him." (Lk 19:4)

Because Zacchaeus knew what Jesus was doing and that He was passing by, he did his best to meet Him. Take some time and, as you become aware of your needs and feelings, answer these questions:

- Who and what speaks to you of Jesus in life?
- What generates in you the desire to see and meet Jesus?
- What weaknesses or strengths urge you to meet Jesus or are you perhaps still indifferent towards Him?
- What is the place and time for you to find, meet and know Jesus?
- Right now, what are you doing to meet and know Jesus more?

The obstacles Zacchaeus faced were his being a short man in the big crowd:

- What are the obstacles that hinder you from getting in touch with Jesus and experiencing His love more closely?

- Are you doing something to overcome these obstacles or are you afraid and do you keep procrastinating?
- Take a few moments and see how you are handling some difficult situations in your life. Ask Jesus to enlighten and strengthen you.

"When Jesus came to the spot He looked up and said, 'Zacchaeus, hurry down. I mean to stay at your house today.'" (Lk 19:5)

The little effort that Zacchaeus made was greatly rewarded. Jesus looked up at him (respected him) and invited Himself to his house. Take a moment to experience the joy that Zacchaeus felt as Jesus accepted him and respected him for who he was.

As you experience this joy, I invite you to choose events or special moments in life when Jesus answered your prayers or needs generously:

- What needs or desires did you want Jesus to fulfill in you?
- How strong were your faith and trust in Jesus as you presented these needs to Him?
- How did Jesus answer your prayer?
- What facts, feelings and thoughts did you then experience as Jesus proved His great love for you?
- For a moment, relive the joy, affirmation and courage you then felt.
- Relish the peace and serenity that your soul and spirit experienced.
- Become aware of how even your body expressed the Lord's visitation to you.
- As you experience Jesus looking at you and inundating you with His love, accepting you as you are, take a couple of moments of silent, loving adoration.

"I give half my belongings, Lord, to the poor. If I have defrauded anyone in the least, I pay him back fourfold." (Lk 19:8)

The result of Jesus accepting Zacchaeus was a sincere change of heart, a making good the wrong that preceded. Look at your life history, especially at the times when Jesus visited you:

- Did these visits of Jesus leave a lasting effect on you?
- Did you experience a spiritual growth, a change of heart?
- Do you still live that change of heart or do you need Jesus to visit you again?
- What does it cost you to remain faithful in following Jesus?

Before you end this exercise, take a moment to relive the visitation of Jesus to your heart. Thank Him for His compassionate love and forgiving understanding and ask Him to continue saving you as you hear Him say to you: ''Today salvation has come to this house.''

42.
THE RICH MAN
(Mark 10:17-27)

AS YOU ENTER into prayer, I invite you to become the rich person in the gospel. The evangelist introduces the youth as a good person seeking greater generosity. ''Good Teacher, what must I do to share in everlasting life?'' Jesus answered, ''You know the commandments . . .'' and he replied to Jesus, ''Teacher, I have kept all these since my childhood.'' (Mk 10:17-21)

This person is young, very rich, morally good, obeys the commandments and desires to do more. In the quietness of your heart, look at yourself and become aware of similarities between this person and you:

- Are you a young person? Youthfulness is not in your age or unwrinkled skin, but in an open spirit, always ready to learn, grow and develop.
- How young do you consider yourself spiritually, physically and emotionally?
- Is this youthfulness an asset, a gift and an honor to you or is it a cause of shame and worry because you have not grown accordingly?
- Are you a rich person? What aspect or aspects in you do you consider enriching?
- Name the riches . . . place them into different categories.
- Do you appreciate your riches? How do you use them?
- "I have kept all these since my childhood." This is how the person in the gospel explained his relationship with God.
- What is your relationship and intimacy with Jesus?
- How do you explain or express it to others: obedience to rules, conformity to traditions, generous zeal for the Kingdom?
- Do you feel satisfied with your spiritual maturity and with the way you use your human riches?
- Spend a few moments taking in all your richness, accepting it and realizing that it is all a gift shared by Jesus with you.

"Then Jesus looked at him with love and told him, 'There is one thing more you must do. Go and sell what you have and give to the poor; you will then have treasure in heaven. After that, come and follow me.' " (Mk 10:21-22)

Jesus loved this man very much and because of this sincere love, He challenged him to take a risk, to make a leap in the dark. Imagine Jesus in front of you, look at His eyes and allow Him to look at you. Let His look penetrate your heart, and experience the depth of His love for you:

- What people, facts and feelings come to your heart and convince you that you are personally loved by Jesus?

- Take a few moments and experience the love of Jesus for you as He keeps looking at you.
- As you experience this love of Jesus, listen to Him telling you, "There is one thing more you must do."
- What is that one thing Jesus is asking you to do that will give you real happiness or true peace of soul?
- Do you like the one thing/action that Jesus is asking you to do?
- How attached are you to it?
- Are you ready to offer it to Jesus or do you have to wait and think about it?
- What price do you have to pay to please Jesus right now? Can you, are you ready, and do you really want to pay this price?
- Ask Jesus to help you detach yourself from your possessions and to help you let go and deepen your trust in Him.

The young person was asked by Jesus to follow Him only after he had given up all his possessions. Become aware of your different possessions and the degrees of attachment you have for them. At this time in your life:

- Is Jesus asking you to let go or give up some dear attachment or possession?
- Is Jesus asking you to be more positive, to become more secure or to purify yourself from some destructive weakness?
- How ready and willing are you to consider every attachment you have as secondary so as to rise and follow Jesus wholeheartedly?
- What obstacles and hindrances prevent you from following Jesus generously?
- Ask Jesus to give you the necessary graces you need.

"At these words the man's face fell. He went away sad, because he had many possessions." (Mk 10:22)   He was unable to advance in holiness because his many riches possessed him. As you look at yourself and experience the attachments within you:

- Do you too turn away from Jesus and become sad because you cannot master your attachment to your riches?
- Are you ready to let go, to give up every human bondage so as to obtain greater spiritual freedom and integrity?
- What gives you courage and determination to say a FULL YES to Jesus?
- Is it your prayer life, your deep faith in God's divine providence or your personal experience of being so much loved by Jesus?

Before you end this exercise, take a few moments of quiet prayer with Jesus:

- Thank Him for all the spiritual strength with which He has blessed you.
- Thank Him for other human qualities and material riches you have.
- Thank Him for the wisdom and prudence you cherish that lead you so near to Him.
- Thank Him especially for His active presence within you as you realize that "with God all things are possible." (Mk 10:27)
- When you are ready, gently end this exercise.

43.
THE RICH FOOL
(Luke 12:13-21)

IMAGINE YOURSELF the rich person that Jesus speaks about in the gospel. Look at yourself and become aware of the riches you possess:

- Qualities, talents, characteristics.
- Skills, practicality, a mechanical mind and hands.
- Intelligence: languages, science, general knowledge.
- Family: spouse and children, love, care, respect, union.
- Job: security, social status.
- Spirituality: faith, religion.

As you get in touch with the richness within you, the beautiful person you are, look at your childhood and become aware of:

- The simple and ordinary beginnings of your life.
- The many people who were involved in the process of your enrichment.
- The part YOU played in using your gifts and cooperating with helpful people.

Now that you have a good feel for the rich person you are:

- Do you think that you would have become what you are today just by yourself?
- To whom and to what are you most indebted?
- What part does Jesus/God play in you becoming the person you are today?

The rich person in the gospel became very attached to riches. He did not want to lose any of them and worked hard to preserve them. Knowing yourself as the rich and beautiful person you are:

- Are you sufficiently aware of, and do you fully accept, your riches?
- Is your attachment to your riches healthy and dependent on God, or is it selfish and leading to destruction?
- Become aware of the attachment to different areas of your riches. Name the healthy ones and be grateful to God.

- Now name the unhealthy or selfish attachments that might cause your ruin.
- What can you do about them?

In this blind possessiveness, the rich person in the gospel became so selfish and earth-bound that he lost all wisdom and prudence in his spiritual dependence on God.

Look at yourself and become aware of your attitudes and behavior at home, at work and in society. When you are in the company of others:

- What are your ordinary thoughts about yourself, about others?
- Do you look down upon others because they are financially poorer than you?
- Do you take for granted those less skilled than you?
- Do you misjudge and criticize those less clever or less practical than you?
- Do you feel superior to others because of your skin color, money or profession?
- Where do you stand in your spiritual riches?
- How do you compare your intellectual and psychological growth and human accumulated riches with your spiritual treasures?

The materially rich person in the gospel was a spiritual pauper. Because of this, God called him a FOOL. He was too attached to what could be taken away from him in a moment.

Take a few moments of prayerful reflection and, before you end the exercise, become aware of:

- The material and spiritual riches you possess.
- The way you appreciate and are attached to each of them.
- Which riches you value most in life, the spiritual or the material.
- The feedback you receive from other people as they relate to you.
- The feelings that are going on within you.

As you end the prayer:

- Thank Jesus for all those things for which you are grateful.
- Ask Him to purify or heal your faulty attachment.
- Place your trust in His loving goodness. As you pray, ask that God will help you to be still richer in His sight rather than piling up material riches that can be taken away from you at any moment.

44.

MARY MAGDALENE
(John 20:1-18)

FOR YOUR PRAYER, I invite you to become Mary Magdalene and experience yourself as a new person having received Christ's forgiveness. As you get in touch with yourself:

- Who were you when you first met Jesus?
- How did Jesus accept you then?
- What did you offer Him and what did He give you in return?
- Feel the joy and peace of Christ's new life in you.
- Experience the urge to develop a strong relationship with Him.

The passion and death of Jesus happened too quickly after you encountered Him. As you accept the reality of Jesus' death, take a moment and:

- Experience the pain of separation and the need to be reunited with Him.

"Early in the morning, while it was still dark, Mary Magdalene came to the tomb." (Jn 20:1)

- Feel the pain of complete loss as you see "that the stone had been moved away." (20:1)
- What is going on within you as you experience loss, separation, pain?
- Why do you run to the disciples to share your loss?
- As Peter and John run to the tomb and you follow them slowly, come in touch with yourself and ask:
- Who is Jesus for me that I miss Him so much?
- Is my relationship with Him over?
- What can I do to renew it, even though it will never be the same again?
- Listen to your feelings and trust your instincts as they urge you to remain near the tomb, seeking your Beloved.

In her desire to keep her relationship with Jesus alive, "Mary stood weeping beside the tomb. Even as she wept, she stooped to peer inside, and there she saw two angels in dazzling robes." (Jn 20:11-12) Mary seeks the Lord even when she is sad and feels the pain of separation when there was little hope of finding or seeing Him again.

Become aware of a couple of events in your life when you lost a dear person, stopped a meaningful friendship or had to give up something that meant much to you. Reliving these events:

- Feel the deep attachment to the person or thing and experience how devastated you felt at the loss.
- At this time, were you angry at God or at others? Did you fall into a crisis of faith?
- Or did you experience an inner strength that offered you patience and wisdom to bear your trial and cross in a redeeming way?
- Spend a moment of quiet prayer and let your heart rest gently in the heart of Jesus.

Mary looked for the Lord and she was greatly rewarded. Jesus came to her and strengthened her for a new life of love in faith by:

1. Renewing friendship with her. "Woman . . . Who is it you are looking for?" (Jn 20:15)

- Were there times in your life when Jesus Himself sought your friendship?
- How did He do this?
- Who and what did Jesus use to attract you to a deeper love and greater friendship?
- Did you then recognize Jesus clearly or did you have to ponder in your heart what was happening?

2. Increasing her yearning for Him. ". . . Jesus said to her, 'Mary!' She turned to Him and said, 'Rabbouni!' " (Jn 20:16)

- In moments of intimacy, by what name does Jesus call you?
- By what name do you call Jesus as you respond?
- Take a moment and relive an experience in life when you heard Jesus calling you by name and you responded with great affection.

3. Preparing her for a new relationship in faith. "Do not cling to Me, for I have not yet ascended to the Father." (Jn 20:17)

- Mary came to believe that her relationship with Jesus had to be on a new level. She learned this:
  - From the loving way that Jesus called her name.
  - From the interior consolation she experienced within her.
  - From the reality that Jesus was truly dead yet really present to her and in her.

As you look at similar experiences within you:

- Can you truly say that your friendship and relationship with Jesus is true, real and personal?

• Thank Jesus for your belief and experience in this personal relationship with Him.

Mary Magdalene was able to personalize this experience as she fulfilled the mission that Jesus gave her. "Mary Magdalene went to the disciples. 'I have seen the Lord!' she announced. Then she reported what He said to her." (Jn 20:18)

Before you end the prayer, take a few moments of reflection and relive some special touch of the Lord that happened during this exercise. Experience the loving friendship that Jesus offers you, thank Him for His love and, as He calls you by name, revere Him by calling Him "Rabbouni."

GUARDIANS

45.
RAPHAEL

(Tobit 7, 11)

I INVITE YOU to let your imagination activate itself as you center your attention on the archangel Raphael. Raphael is not a human being but an angel:

- Are you aware that the Scriptures speak of good and bad angels?
- Do you believe in the angels, and what is the basis of your belief?
- What is your personal experience of angels?
- Take a moment and express this experience to yourself in words.

The word "angel" means "messenger," and God uses these messengers when He wants to communicate some important truth or reality to us. Angels do not have a body. They are pure spirit and, like us humans, they are created by and dependent on God.

I invite you to look at your life and become aware of your spiritual growth:

- Have you ever experienced a message personally addressed to you?
- Who or what was the messenger?
- Was the "angel" an inspiration, a good friend, an accident or some other event?

- Were you aware of the messenger from the beginning or did you need time to recognize him/her/it?
- Can you truthfully say that these messengers were God-sent, specially chosen for you?
- What was your response to God's message and what reactions did you have to the messengers?
- Choose one experience in life when Jesus gave you special news through a messenger. Become aware of who or what was the messenger, or the content of the message and of the process of your response. As you do this, be grateful to Jesus and talk to Him about your belief in His messengers.

The proper name given to angels describes their ministry. Raphael means ''Healing of God,'' because this is what he brought to Sarah and Tobit.

Sarah was married seven times and each husband died before he slept with her. (Tob 3:7-8)   On Raphael's advice, Sarah was delivered from this curse and was happily married to Tobiah all the rest of her life. (Tob 7:12-8:3)

Tobit was blind for eight years and through Raphael's message, he was healed and could see again. (Tob 11:7-14)

Both Sarah and Tobit experienced God's healing through the angel. They believed in God's messenger, accepted the message and as a result were healed. Take a few moments and become aware of:

- How many times you have experienced ''the healing of God'' in your life?
- Was this healing physical, moral, emotional, psychological?
- Who or what was the Raphael, the messenger of healing to you?
- What obstacles prevented you from accepting God's healing promptly?
- Who and what encouraged you to experience God's healing?

- Take a moment and, as you go through a meaningful healing experience in life, thank Jesus for the Raphaels in your life and for all the healing with which God has blessed you.

Now I invite you to become aware of a couple of occasions when YOU were a Raphael to others and when you were used as God's messenger bringing healing:

- To whom and where were you sent?
- What were the circumstances?
- What message did you communicate and how did you do it?
- What response did the message get?
- What was the profit you and the other person gained from the healing offered?
- Was this profit spiritual, moral, emotional, physical?
- Thank Jesus for choosing you to be His messenger of compassion, healing and forgiveness. Compare yourself with Raphael as an instrument of healing, come near to Jesus and ask Him to make you a purer messenger of His loving healing. When you are ready, gently end the exercise.

46.
GABRIEL
(Luke 1, Daniel 8-9)

IN YOUR PRAYER, let your imagination activate itself as you center your attention on the archangel Gabriel. Gabriel is a created spirit and is called an archangel because his mission was to announce the greatest news ever given.

Like Raphael and Michael, Gabriel is a messenger of God, sent with a mission. Gabriel means "Strength of God." His mission is to communicate to us that God's strength is to be shared with us humans. This strength does not only mean power but is also richness in mercy, plenitude of grace and source of life:

- What feelings and emotions arise in your heart as you feel the strength of God in you?
- What thoughts and ideas fill your mind as you reflect on God's strength shared with you?
- What attitudes does this strength reflect in you?

  - Glory, praise, honor, joy and closeness?
  - Or fear, timidity, weakness and distance?

- Have you ever experienced the strength of God? Where? How? When?
- What is the fruit of this strength of God in you?

"Your prayer has been heard. Your wife Elizabeth shall bear a son whom you shall name John. Joy and gladness will be yours, and many will rejoice at his birth . . . I am Gabriel, who stand in attendance before God. I was sent to speak to you and bring you this good news." (Lk 1:13-14, 19)

Gabriel announces to Zechariah that his sterile wife will conceive in her old age. Because of his unbelief, Zechariah was silenced until the birth of his son, John. As you look at your life:

- Have you ever experienced disbelief or discouragement because you were truly aware of your weakness and limitations?
- In the challenges you faced and the risks you took, how did the strength of God show itself in you?
- Who or what was the Gabriel that instilled courage in you to accept and cooperate with the strength of God?

• Thank Jesus for an experience when you felt this energizing strength in you.

"The angel Gabriel was sent from God . . . to a virgin . . . [named] Mary . . . the angel said to her . . . 'You have found favor with God . . . You shall conceive and bear a son and give Him the name Jesus . . . and the power of the Most High will overshadow you.' " (Lk 1:26-35)

The all-powerful Lord announced to Mary that He chose to dwell within her to become human to save us from sin. What a marvel of grace! Mary, a young woman experiences this marvel and asks, "How can this be?" (Lk 1:34)

Get in touch with your true self, blessed and graced yet weak and limited:

• When, in your life, has Jesus found favor in you?
• What qualities, gifts and virtues made Jesus favor you?
• For what mission did Jesus favor you?
• Was your response similar or different from Mary's?
• What made YOU say "Yes, let it be to me as you say"?
• Take some time for humble and grateful dialogue with the divine strength of your life.

"Gabriel . . . came to me . . . 'Daniel, I have now come to give you understanding. When you began your prayer, an answer was given which I have come to announce, because you are beloved. Therefore mark the answer and understand the vision.' " (Dn 9:22-23)

Gabriel brought an understanding of various visions to Daniel. Without God's strength (gifts), Daniel could not help his people turn away from sin and deepen their hope in a peaceful future.

I invite you to get in touch with your wisdom and intelligence and the way you have used these gifts in life:

- Are you aware of events in life when you acted or said the right thing because wisdom and understanding were given to you from above?
- Choose one such event and:
  - Become aware of your human, limited knowledge of the person and situation.
  - Then get in touch with your listening capacity and the love you placed in this listening.
  - Recognize the moment when wisdom and understanding were given to you by God.
  - Reflect on the fruit of this God-given wisdom in you and in the other person.
  - As you do this, take some time for loving conversation with Jesus and thank Him for His strength shared with you in different areas of your life. When you are ready, gently end the exercise.

47.

MICHAEL

(Revelation 12:7; Daniel 10, 12)

I INVITE YOU to let your imagination activate itself as you center your attention on the archangel Michael. Michael, like Raphael and Gabriel, is a created angel, God's special messenger, communicating to us God's omnipotence.

The name Michael means "Who is like God" and his mission is to announce that God is all-powerful. By name and action, Michael makes known to us that no created being can equal or overcome God's power.

In the Book of Revelation, Michael is presented as waging war with the Evil Spirit who seeks to destroy the Woman (symbol for the New Jerusalem) and her newborn child (Jesus, the Messiah).

"Then war broke out in heaven; Michael and his angels battled against the dragon." (Rev. 12:7)

Michael is God's faithful defender. Because he acknowledged God's supremacy and his total dependence on God, Michael and his angels fought strongly against pride and insubordination.

As you reflect on your faith-life and religious beliefs:

- How strong is your faith in an omnipotent God and in Jesus, His Son?
- What brought you to this deep-founded faith?
- What gifts, strengths and qualities led you to deepen this intimacy with the Triune God?
- What evils and weakness had you to fight against?
- Where and how strongly do you experience the Michael (Who is like God) in you?
- As you go through the struggle of growth in faith, thank Jesus for His love for you and ask Him to strengthen your will-power to fight the evils that seek to destroy you.

"Soon I must fight the prince of Persia again. When I leave, the prince of Greece will come. No one supports me against all these except Michael, standing as a reenforcement and a bulwark for me." (Dn 10:21)

"At that time, there shall arise Michael, the great prince, guardian of your people." (Dn 12:1)

In the Book of Daniel, Michael is presented as a guardian defending Israel in its time of trouble. This trouble was very much religious since Michael wages war against the forces of evil that sought to destroy the name of Yahweh from Israel.

I invite you to get in touch with your spiritual journey — your growth in knowing, loving and accepting Jesus in your life. In this journey:

- What are the evils, selfish desires, weaknesses and people you had to fight against?
- How strong were you in faith?
- How convinced were you that Jesus will fight with and in you?
- How did you experience the Lord's effective power in you?
- Was it your well-founded faith . . . a holy person . . . a special event in life that convinced you that "the Almighty has done great things for me"? (cf. Lk 1:49)
- Who are the Michaels in your life that fought with you, stood by your religious beliefs and guarded you against spiritual and moral pitfalls?
- Take a few moments and, as these Michaels come to your heart and mind, offer them to the Lord, thank Him for their strength and ask Him to draw you nearer to His heart.

I now invite you to look at your love for and faith in Jesus. As you become aware of the depth of your intimacy with Jesus, your rock and salvation, reflect on your life and ask yourself:

- Did I ever wage war to defend and make holy the name and person of Jesus?
- What did these wars cost me:
  - Physical and emotional pain?
  - Perhaps loss of friends or a job?
- Am I satisfied with the way I witness to my love for Jesus?
- Am I equally strong in my defense of the Church and its teachings?
- Or do I seek soft cushions because of some deep-seated wound?

- How do I reconcile my faith in and love for Jesus, His Church and my neighbor?

Before you end the exercise take a few moments of faith-filled dialogue with Jesus. Thank Him for the Michaels in your life. Thank Him for the many times that He used you as a Michael (Who is like God) to others. Ask Him to continue strengthening you in your war against every evil. When you are ready, gently end the exercise.

48.

GUARDIAN ANGEL
(Psalm 91; Matthew 18:10; Acts 10, 12)

SCRIPTURE SPEAKS of angels as God's messengers and ministers. It is a Christian belief that God entrusts every human being to the guidance and protection of an angel.

I invite you to look at your life as a journey that you are experiencing with your guardian angel. As you do this:

- Do you really believe that God entrusted your whole life to one of His angels?
- Are you aware of the presence of a guardian angel in your life?
- Is this awareness based only on belief or also on personal experiences of guidance and protection?
- What relationship do you have with your guardian angel?
- Do you take your angel for granted . . . seek guidance and protection . . . ask for help . . . are grateful for what your angel does for you?
- If you do not believe in a guardian angel, reflect for a moment and see if you are missing something in life.

"See, I am sending an angel before you to guard you on the way and bring you to the place I have prepared for you. Be attentive to him and heed his voice." (Ex 23:20-21)

God gave this promise to Moses, to the Chosen People and to all the People of God:

- Do you experience this promise fulfilled in you?
- Become aware of the ways your angel guarded you at every stage of your growth.
- How was this guidance given to you?

1. Was it through an INSPIRATION, a strong feeling, a meaningful dream? ". . . he had a vision in which he clearly saw a messenger of God coming toward him and calling, 'Cornelius . . . Your prayers and your generosity have risen in God's sight, and because of them, he has remembered you.' " (Ac 10:3-4)

- If this is so with you, relive in imagination events when you were sure that what you did was highly influenced by your guardian angel. Be grateful and renew your trust in his inspiration.

2. Was it through a CORRECTION, perhaps remorse of conscience or a healthy guilt-feeling? "Upon their hands they shall bear you up, lest you dash your foot against a stone." (Ps 91:12)

- If you have experienced this, thank the Creator for giving you such a companion-friend.
- As you do this, become aware of events in your life when you felt the pain and shame of correction together with the newness of purification.
- As you show reverence to your guardian angel, ask her/him to continue guiding your steps as you journey toward eternity.

3. Was it through an ENCOURAGEMENT, a clear order, a success, a conviction?

". . . an angel of the Lord opened the gates of the jail, led them forth, and said, 'Go out now and take your place in the temple precincts and preach to the people all about this new life.' " (Ac 5:19-20)

- Let such convincing events in your life unfold themselves to you.
- Experience again God's power in you, ministered through His angel.
- Be grateful to God and your angel for the strength they offer you to grow.

The mission of the guardian angel is not only to guide, but also to protect you from every harm. "No evil shall befall you, nor shall affliction come near your tent. For to His angels He has given command about you, that they guard you in all your ways. Upon their hands they shall bear you up lest you dash your foot against a stone." (Ps 91:10-12)

Once more become aware of your life journey:

- Have you ever experienced yourself protected from evil by your guardian angel?
- What were the evils you were protected from: moral, physical, spiritual?
- What convinces you that it was the angel's care that protected you from these harms and evils?
- Were you immediately aware of this or did you need time to realize it?
- Thank God and His angel for this protection and ask them to continue shielding you from harm and evil.

God tells you, together with the Chosen People, "Be attentive to the angel and heed his voice." (Ex 23:21)

As you look at your life:

- Are you satisfied with your cooperation with your guardian angel?
- How attentive are you to the given guidance?
- How much time and attention do you give to the angel's voice within you?
- What place does the guardian angel have in your heart?

While acknowledging the active presence of your guardian angel within you:

- Show reverence for the Spirit's presence in you.
- Strengthen your trust in the angel's wise guidance and powerful protection.
- Improve your devotion to your angel because of the loving care you are given.

Before you end this exercise, take a few moments of intimate prayer with your guardian angel:

- Be grateful for all the angel does for you.
- Ask for a continued friendship till the end of your life.

49.
CROWNED WITH GLORY
AND HONOR

(Psalm 8)

TODAY I invite you to pray joyfully and gratefully as you allow your imagination to unfold to you all the riches you have discovered within you as you prayed the preceding exercises. As you do this, join the Psalmist and sing: "How glorious is Your name, O Lord, over all the earth." (Ps 8:1)

- What feelings move you to praise and glorify the Lord's name?
- What people, positive events and memories allow these feelings to arise within you?
- What qualities, strengths, virtues and gifts have you discovered as forming you into the beautiful person you are?
- What grace or gift leads you to burst into your joyful song of praise?

"Out of the mouth of babes . . . you have fashioned praise . . . to silence the hostile and the vengeful." (Ps 8:3)

You are aware of your strengths, beauty and richness. Accepting it all is too humbling an experience. As you look into your life:

- Who are the babes that recognize your richness and simply proclaim it to others?
- Are these babes friends, people you rarely meet, little children, broken people?
- Are there "hostile and vengeful" people in your life?
- What makes these people "hostile and vengeful" to you?
- How does the recognition and affirmation of your richness silence these "hostile and vengeful" people?

"When I behold the heavens, the work of your fingers . . . what am I that You should be mindful of me?" (Ps 8:4-5)

Looking at the beautiful sky and admiring the wonder of nature, you are forced to look at and admire the gift of yourself, even though it is imperfect:

- What weaknesses, limitations and imperfections make you proclaim this statement?
- What specific moments or events of spiritual or moral growth make you aware that Jesus is mindful of you?
- What people made you aware that Jesus is caring for you through what they have done for or with you?
- Take a few moments and let these people and their actions open your mind to marvel at and your heart to glorify God's mindfulness and care for you.

"You have made him little less than the angels and crowned him with glory and honor." (Ps 8:6)

You know that the angels are God's special messengers entrusted with special missions:

- What makes you say to God that you are a "little less than the angels"?
- Is it your spiritual growth, your integrated personality, your accumulated wisdom and experiences?
- How and with what has Jesus crowned you with glory and honor?
- What is it that makes you honorable and glorified in life?
- Take a moment of prayer to honor and praise God for sharing these gifts with you.

"You have given him rule over the works of your hands, putting all things under his feet." (Ps 8:7)

We all rejoice when things go well and when we have a certain control and knowledge of things:

- What are the "works of His hands" that God entrusted to your rule?
- In what way do you possess a ruling over these works?
- How have you used your prudence and wisdom in ruling over the works of the Lord?

- Are these "works of the Lord" your family, co-workers, people for whom you are responsible?
- Are addicts, prostitutes, unemployed, rejected and unloved people included in these "works of the Lord"?
- What skills, profession or talents has the Lord offered you for your possession?
- What is your attitude toward "putting all things under my feet"?
- Is it a means that leads you to humility, loving service and trustworthy care?
- Or does it lead you to pride, hard-heartedness and self-destruction?

Before you end the exercise, listen once more to the song of creation and to the praise of all creatures. Then turn to the Lord, your God, Master and Creator and, as you rejoice in the masterpiece He helped you to become, end the prayer by repeating joyfully, honestly and humbly:

"How glorious is your name, O Lord, over all the earth . . . You crowned me with glory and honor."

50.
BE ON YOUR GUARD
(Luke 21:34-38)

ON THE LAST DAY of the liturgical year, Jesus advises us to be on our guard. In the liturgical year, the life and mission of Jesus blesses us with the awareness of our strengths and weaknesses. So also the praying of the preceding exercises brings us to the realization of who we are and what we value. For this last prayer, I invite you to let Jesus touch you with His invitation to "be on your guard." (Lk 21:34)

Imagine Jesus standing in front of you. Look at Him and take in all the details of His personality. Let your heart meet His heart and experience the feelings and attitudes of Jesus toward you.

As a caring parent or a loving brother, Jesus shares His concern for you: "Be on guard lest your spirits become bloated with indulgence and drunkenness." (Lk 21:34) Looking at your lifestyle:

- Where do you naturally and ordinarily place your attention?
- Are you ordinarily occupied with feasting, pleasure-seeking, self-satisfaction?
- Or do you use joyful occasions for your growth in a healthy way?
- Is alcohol or drugs an addiction for you?
- Or do you consume alcohol with moderation and temperance?
- In celebrations, do your heart and mind act prudently or do you give in completely to your bodily cravings and lusts?

"Be on guard lest your spirits become bloated with . . . worldly cares." (Lk 21:34) Look at an ordinary day or week in your life:

- What percentage of each day is given to human respect, recognition or trying to impress others?
- How much do you worry about past behavior and impressions?
- Name some of the anxieties that burden your heart during the day.
- Are you ever anxious or worried about spiritual growth or your intimacy with Jesus/God?
- How do social injustices, global inequality and pain because of color, race, or religion affect you?
- What do you hear Jesus telling you right now?
- What is your response to Him?

"The great day will suddenly close in on you like a trap."
(Lk 21:34)   In your quiet moments:

- Do you ever think of the day when God will call you to eternal life?
- Does the thought of this day bring you peace, calmness and hope or does it fill you with anxiety, worry and fear?
- Or does the afterlife have no place in your heart?
- Take a few moments, listen to Jesus telling you this statement again and become aware of the feelings arising within you.

"So be on the watch. Pray constantly for the strength to escape whatever is in prospect." (Lk 21:36)

Jesus offers you the advice to watch and pray. In your relationship with others, at home and at work:

- Do you naturally and ordinarily see yourself as loving, doing good, helping and being compassionate?
- Or are you selfish, self-centered and withdrawn?
- What value and importance do you give to prayer?
- Do you have a discipline of daily prayer, a time and space for yourself and your God?
- Or is prayer the last item on your priority list and frequently given up?

Prayer is important in life. It gives you the strength to safely experience whatever happens and it prepares you "to stand secure before the Son of Man." (Lk 21:36)

- Are you aware that faith-filled prayer makes easier the burden of pain and sorrow and enhances the joy of experiencing God's living love for you?
- Do you turn to God/Jesus in gratitude, trust and hope when good and bad things happen to you?

- Relive in imagination a good and bad experience and feel again the fruit of God's grace in you because you had recourse to prayer.

Before you end the prayer, take a few moments of loving dialogue with Jesus.

- Offer Him your self with all its strengths and weaknesses.
- Ask Him to continue drawing you nearer to His heart and to give you the grace to realize that what you are doing in faith now is really preparing you "to stand secure before the Son of Man" when you are called to eternal life.